Praise for *Get What You Want*

"Julie Solomon has a profound calling for helping people to conquer their feelings of powerlessness. One of her truly unique gifts is helping people step into becoming all that they are meant to be so that they can experience the full freedom that life has to offer. Read this book to find out how to do that for yourself!"
—RORY VADEN,
cofounder of Brand Builders Group and
New York Times bestselling author of *Take the Stairs*

"Julie has personally helped me release shame and live fully and walk freely in my story. She instilled in me a rhythm of learning from the past, goalsetting, and boundary making, which have ultimately created a clarity in my vision for my purpose for life. This is a must-read to learn these skills to press forward in a newfound strength!"
—LAUREN KENNEDY,
New York Times bestselling author of *Still Lolo*

"*Get What You Want* is exactly what it sounds like, plus a ton of kickass advice and serious empowerment you might not expect. The fact that this book is this good AND coming from a powerful woman in a niche often dominated by men makes it an absolute must-read. Cannot recommend this enough!"
—ALLIE CASAZZA,
bestselling author of *Declutter Like A Mother* and
host of the chart-topping podcast *The Purpose Show*

"If you have big plans to be, do, and have MORE—let it be easy by following Julie's words that are more valuable than gold."
—SUSIE MOORE,
bestselling author of *Let It Be Easy*

"In *Get What You Want*, Julie does such a beautiful job inviting us into the process of remembering our worthiness and releasing so many of our conditioned limiting beliefs in a way that is accessible and inviting so that we can begin telling a new, empowered story in our lives."
—RUTHIE LINDSEY,
speaker, activist, and author

"When it comes to getting what you want, Julie Solomon really knows what it takes and vulnerably and generously shares it. Her stories and methods will inspire you, move you, and give you just the jolt you need to believe in yourself and your dreams, and take powerful, courageous action. Hers is the voice you need in your head when you're looking at your vision board asking, 'But how??' Read this book and change your life! You won't regret it."
—JAMIE JENSEN,
award-winning writer and producer

JULIE SOLOMON

Get What You Want

HOW TO GO FROM UNSEEN
TO UNSTOPPABLE

HarperCollins
Leadership

An Imprint of HarperCollins

Published by HarperCollins Leadership, an imprint of HarperCollins Focus LLC.

Any internet addresses, phone numbers, or company or product information printed in this book are offered as a resource and are not intended in any way to be or to imply an endorsement by HarperCollins Leadership, nor does HarperCollins Leadership vouch for the existence, content, or services of these sites, phone numbers, companies, or products beyond the life of this book.

ISBN 978-1-4002-2618-4 (eBook)
ISBN 978-1-4002-2617-7 (HC)

Library of Congress Cataloging-in-Publication Data
Library of Congress Cataloging-in-Publication application has been submitted.

Printed in the United States of America
22 23 24 25 26 LSC 10 9 8 7 6 5 4 3 2 1

FOR CAMDEN AND LILY JO,

may you always believe that anything is possible.

AND FOR JOHN,

who has always believed in my possibility.

CONTENTS

PART THREE

The Results

PROLOGUE

A COUPLE OF YEARS AGO, I got my copy of a new book from one of my favorite female entrepreneurs. Years earlier I had learned that she was one of the very first female entrepreneurs who was doing exactly what I wanted to do in business. She had served hundreds of thousands of women across the globe, made millions of dollars empowering other women to do the same, supported incredible charities, and spoke on some of the most sought-after stages. This woman was unstoppable.

I was excited to sit down and sink my time and energy into her brand-new, widely anticipated book. I couldn't wait to learn new business strategies and hear her take on how to overcome life's challenges and become successful. But most important, I was excited to get to know her. I wanted to know about her struggles, her vulnerable moments, her trials and tribulations, with the hope that, maybe, I would see a piece of myself in her and not feel so alone.

As I began to read her book, I quickly realized that almost everything in it was just transcriptions of her past speaking engagements, webinars, and online programs. At this point, I knew this woman's work so well that I started to paraphrase what was coming in the next chapters before I even got there. I made it about a quarter of the way through, put the book on my bookshelf, and never opened it again. I was underwhelmed. I had wanted so much more. I had wanted *her.*

I knew that if I was ever given the opportunity to write a book (and actually have people read the damn thing, no less), I would make sure to bring the one thing that I want when I read a book: authenticity.

Here's the truth: I've never written a book. I was never taught how to write a book. I'm the absolute worst at grammar, and don't know the first thing about editing. But I do know what it's like to have the desire to share your story. I do know the impact of seeing yourself in someone else that goes beyond a curated Instagram picture. I do know what it feels like to want more from a leader you admire than the generalized "just be yourself" statements (if it were that easy, this book wouldn't exist).

Most important, I do know the courage you can gain from seeing someone else do something you've always wanted to do.

And that is why this book exists. This book contains completely new, personal material, in a way that I have never shared before. For some of you, this information may be shocking based on my persona or what you're used to seeing from me. For others, it may be the warm, welcomed hug that you've wanted me to share for some time now.

I poured my heart into this book because I wanted to give you the authentic me. This isn't to say that my podcast and my coaching aren't authentic, but I've always had a bit of a "let's focus down and get shit done" energy between me and my community because I pride myself on being results-focused. But I'm discovering that results can also come from being vulnerable and sharing more of my genuine self.

For our time together here, I've torn those walls down to share my experience, with the intention that it gives you the strength and hope to do the same in your own lives. You can't get what you want until you know what you want. And in order to know what you want, you need to be honest with yourself. It took me a long time to pinpoint who I wanted to be and what I wanted to do. This isn't a story about overnight success. This is the story of a woman who found out what was holding her back and created a new path to get what she wanted and got it.

I'm sharing with you what I've gone through, because perhaps you have gone through some of these things too. And maybe there is something to be learned and shared here.

My goal with this book is to help anyone get what they want in life—especially those who think getting what they want is impossible. I know what that feels like. I was once there too. And I am here to say, it's possible. *You* are possible. I'd love for you to join me.

Yours,

Julie

INTRODUCTION

"Supposed To" Means Crap

"HEY, HON!" SAID MY HUSBAND through the phone in a maddeningly chipper voice as he was walking into an important meeting with a director. "When were you going to tell me about the credit card?"

I sat at the dining room table, frozen. I had just one frantic thought, over and over: *How do I fix this? How do I fix this?*

My husband had just found out that I'd been hiding $30,000 worth of credit card debt from him. And by "just found out," I mean literally five minutes before the call.

I had to pull myself together and deal with this somehow. But what I really wanted to do was hang up the damn phone, grab some Pirate's Booty, and watch an entire season of *The Real Housewives of Beverly Hills* while letting my denial and delusion freak flags fly with reckless abandon.

Instead, I sat at my dining room table desperately sorting through my thoughts, trying to find my escape hatch. I'd been hiding for two years about amassing $30,000 in credit card debt. I'd justified it by believing it would all be okay. I'd even prepared responses. All of them escaped my memory now.

"I guess now's not the time to tell you that we have more than enough airline points to finally take that trip to Hawaii we've been talking about?" *Ding ding ding. The liar's got a solution!*

Too soon?

"Unfortunately, no." I could hear the anger and hurt in his voice as he saw through my desire to deflect the conversation.

You see, it wasn't supposed to be this way. I was supposed to land a big PR campaign or start doubling down on my content creation that would bring in the big bucks. He was supposed to land a new role in a movie or TV show. I was supposed to win the lottery and get that thing paid off before he knew about it and everything would be fine.

Supposed to means crap.

I do know this: When the spending started two years earlier, I had recently moved to Los Angeles. I didn't have many friends. Throw in the fact that I had a newborn baby boy in tow with no support system, and a new husband who was across the country working. No one told me that the road to finding myself again was going to be a winding, complex one. No one said that after becoming a mother, part of me would die, peacefully and quietly. I didn't know I would miss the part of me that was carefree, independent, and a bit of a wild child. No one told me that through navigating the greatest love I've ever known, and learning every day how to nurture life, I might feel my own self slip through the cracks, a little at a time. No one told me that while stepping into this role called motherhood it was okay to mourn who I had been before. I didn't know what it meant to be a good mother. In sum, I didn't have the tools to handle what was happening. So spending became a way of coping and feeling connected to something greater than myself.

However, I remember being bombarded with the not-so-subtle messages from social media, telling me what it meant to be the perfect mother. I internalized these messages and knew I had to "look the part." I wanted to be fit, have the right clothes, know the right people, and keep up with the Kardashians.

To do this cost a lot of money. $30,000, in fact.

Before I knew it I was filling the emptiness inside myself with "stuff" from outside myself. It hit my pleasure center and made me feel good, temporarily. If you are low—whether you are post-partum, lonely, or sad, especially if you don't feel like you belong or have a purpose that is your own—you're not getting that oxy-tocin hit every day.

So, guess what's going to feel really good? A package in the mail and a really nice lip gloss! I also loved the community and social-ization around shopping. I loved going into a store and having a connection with other women. I finally felt seen and heard from someone other than a baby, and I felt good about myself making a purchase.

And all those "little" interactions and "daily" hits added up to a big pile of debt.

For two years I swore that I had it all under control. And by "having it under control" I mean I buried my head in the sand, rationalizing and justifying my behavior by thinking it would all work itself out. *Was I insane?*

———

You know how a self-righteous woman dies?

She climbs to the top of her ego and jumps off!

I really needed to be right, but self-righteousness would not be my safety net.

I could feel myself becoming more and more aerodynamic as I was metaphorically crashing my way down to a new rock bottom.

So what I wanted was for my Call-Me-on-My-Shit Husband to give me a minute, because things were kind of messed up. I was normally really good at these things. *These things* were faking it till I made it, while forcing whatever solution was necessary so as to not feel pain or discomfort.

Why? Well, it's simple. It's how I learned to survive.

John kept talking, and I honestly had no idea what he was saying. All I kept hearing was my own inner voice asking, *Why am I so afraid to be honest?*

MY MONEY STORY

Up until that point in my life, I had been uncomfortable when it came to money. I was afraid of it, to be honest. I had never been good at math, so when it came time to learn about numbers and finances, I lacked the confidence to take control. Those insecurities were compounded by the fact that I didn't grow up with a lot of money. My parents basically lived paycheck to paycheck when I was young, so topics like "savings" and "investing" and "financial independence" didn't apply to us. I didn't know what a 401(k) was, or how the stock market worked. I remembered sitting in my grandmother's double-wide trailer, watching an infomercial featuring a guy who looked like a cheesy version of Tom Selleck talking about "Financial Freedom for America." I wondered, *How on earth could "making money while you sleep" be possible?*

Success and money became interchangeable in my little-girl mind. When my parents got divorced, my mom was left with two mouths to feed and very little in the way of job qualifications. She had to figure it out and things were difficult for quite a while. Our budgets were held together with a fraying string, and she played Russian roulette with every bill she paid. But my mom was resourceful, and she figured out how to stretch each dollar around the neighborhood and back to make things work. She would work a lot, traveling throughout Tennessee and Kentucky weekly for her pharmaceutical sales job to make sure we had what we needed.

But it wasn't like my dad was really any better off. He worked at an automobile manufacturing plant and lived what we're all told is the American Dream. But to him, having a steady job for thirty years felt like power compared to his parents, who had elementary-school educations, worked odd jobs, and lived in extreme poverty their entire lives.

So much of my childhood was defined by this "lack" mindset. There was never enough money to go around, and the lack of money always caused uncomfortable memories like my mom rushing through the front door to hide her shopping bags in the closet (a pattern that I also picked up in my adult life), the late-night screaming matches that would soothe me to sleep at night, and the ultimate demise of my parents' marriage.

It was difficult for me to be open to the idea of learning how money works and how to make more of it. These beliefs also allowed for years of irrational thinking. I spent decades of my life thinking, *I don't need to understand my finances. My husband/ accountant/Fairy Godmother will deal with all of that.*

I spent years ignoring an extremely important part of my life: money. Truthfully, it wasn't laziness or complacency that drove the decision to avoid what I didn't know. It was fear. Every time I looked at a financial statement and didn't understand it, that voice in my head—you know, the one that sounds like Regina George from *Mean Girls* and likes to point out all your flaws—would list out all the things I was deeply worried about: *You're too dumb to understand this. You're not mature enough with money to figure this out. You need to have someone else handle this for you because you're a financial toddler.* Rather than face it, I ignored it.

I followed what I describe as the small-town mentality. Basically, as long as I had enough to cover my bills on time, most of the time, I just didn't dig any deeper. I felt powerless and helpless when it came to understanding money, let alone being able to have normal conversations about it. And I chose to believe that if I just did X, Y, and Z, my life would work out. I read books about manifesting money. I kept saying to myself, *If you just believe it, you'll achieve it!* And I got really good at working on multiple passions at a time, to try to make the money I needed and wanted.

Years turned into decades of modeling and shaping my relationship with money, success, and freedom, ultimately creating the perfect storm of a narrative—small-town girl meets limiting beliefs and rides off into the sunset with her excuses—that would carry me to this very moment with my husband.

So there I was, at my dining room table, wanting to lie myself out of a $30,000 hole, realizing that if I didn't make some serious changes soon, if I didn't start believing in something greater than myself, my life would crumble beyond repair.

"So," John said. "I don't know what is going on, and I don't have the answers. I am angry, upset, and sad. I don't know if this is an isolated event or if there is a deeper issue here. I am really worried about you. It doesn't feel safe to trust you right now. You need to figure this out because this can't happen again. This is not okay." And he was right. But what *was* okay?

What was possible?

Was it possible to acknowledge my role in this and how I got there? Was it possible to think differently? Was it possible to take responsibility? Was it possible to keep the focus on myself and start taking some honest and real action to achieve the results I wanted in my life?

What did I want? Truly? What was I doing with my life?

For years I thought that once I got the job, or the guy, or the house (or whatever else—fill in the blank), then I'd have the life I always wanted.

That was a lie.

You see, I believed that having to wait for my externals to change before I could move ahead in life was why it was so hard for me to experience success. This belief allowed me to make excuses, and for years, to not take responsibility for my results.

This wasn't the last time we discussed this. But at that moment, John had to go into his meeting. He ended the call with a direct, "I'm taking money from our savings to cover the debt, so it doesn't affect our credit. You'll have to pay us back, in full." I was left thinking, *What am I going to do? How am I going to solve this?*

It was then, feeling completely frozen in this moment, that I made a promise to myself. I promised I would never, ever find myself in this position again, feeling powerless and helpless. I didn't want to feel this guilt and shame or have to make these justifications ever again.

Even though I didn't know how, even though I couldn't control the outcome, I knew that a change was going to come. As one of my favorite authors, Elizabeth Gilbert, shared, "I've never seen any life transformation that didn't begin with the person in question finally getting tired of their own bullshit."

And that was it. I didn't want to keep escaping or trying to fix things. I wanted freedom, confidence, and authenticity. I was going to start on a path of figuring it out.

This was one of the first times that I surrendered to not knowing.

THE CHANGES THAT MADE ME

When I close my eyes now and picture success, I see myself doing work that I love and am excited about, spending time with my family, helping other women lead powerful lives, living in a comfortable house, resting deeply, and being content and joyful in everything I do. And when I open my eyes, that's exactly what I see now. My vision is my reality. It can be yours too.

In this book, I'm going to show you how much you haven't considered. I'm going to invite you to come out of the well-intended haze you may have grown up in to see it for what it really is.

Your belief of what is possible for your own life has been based on what happened in the past. Yet all your possibility is ahead of you. The most basic truth is that getting what you want is about understanding that what is possible for your future may be impossible for you right now, and that impossibility is temporary.

So many of my coaching clients reveal to me that they never thought they could be authors, experts, millionaires, and leaders in their field, all while having happy relationships with their spouses and healthy relationships with their children.

It's not that they tried to be these things and failed. The tragedy is that for decades, they didn't even consider trying. They didn't know what they didn't know. And if we don't know, we can't take action. And we certainly will never get what we want.

Our choices create our actions,

which ultimately create our results.

HOW THIS BOOK
WILL WORK FOR YOU

Since that moment at the dining room table, hearing the shock and concern in my husband's voice, and feeling my own inner world crumbling, I went through a series of actionable steps to live a new life that held my shame with loving compassion and was full of everything I wanted. These are the exact steps that will absolutely work for you, too, if you have the courage to try. If you do the things I teach you in this book, you can achieve anything you want. And I can prove it. I have countless clients who have used these tools to achieve success they never thought possible. You'll be meeting some of them in these pages. This book is divided into three parts.

Part One: Realizing the Possibility

That day at the dining room table, I had to admit what was holding me back, so I could get my mindset right. By the time you're finished reading this book, you, too, will have discovered the beliefs that have been holding you back until now, and all the possibilities that are open to you if you're willing to face the uncomfortable truth. I'll start by teaching you about the belief systems you need to adopt and use to replace whatever is currently keeping you stuck and powerless. I will introduce these belief systems, tell you why they are true, and explain why you must believe them.

Now, I must warn you, you might be resistant to some of these beliefs.

They may be quite simple, but they aren't always easy to accept. If they were, everyone would already have exactly what they wanted.

But in order to step out of the mass production of complacency, you're going to have to stretch yourself to think and feel differently.

Instead of thinking that nothing works for you or that you already know it all, you must ask yourself how this can work for you. What is new that you can learn and apply?

Part Two: Taking Action

Next, I'll teach you what I learned about taking the right kind of action and the knowledge required to do so. I'll show you everything you need to know about how to find balance and apply structure to your goals, using the tools and practices that I have used to coach thousands of people just like you. Finally, I will help you find your unique purpose in life and how to use that purpose in the service of others as someone with massive impact and influence. I'll take you along my own hard-fought and hard-won journey to discovering what my purpose is, and how I use it to help serve others on their own path to success. I'll walk you through the tools and steps of how to go from where you are now to exactly where you want to be. These are the tools and the practices that you will need to do over and over to create action.

Change the way you think, and you'll

ultimately change your life.

As you begin to recognize that you may have been wrong about a lot of things, you will go through what I call a "resistance spin."

It's not enjoyable, but it's a necessary part of the process. It's a true identity crisis. Your brain will want to resist to keep you safe. You will have to overcome those thoughts so you can grow. As you let go of one belief structure, you'll accept a new one that will produce more possibilities. I'll remind you of the actions to take and what to do if you forget and veer off track. Even when you want to quit, I will remind you of what is possible and how important it is in the next part.

Part Three: The Results

I will share inspiring stories of some of my most successful clients who follow this exact process to get what they want. What I love most about these stories is that the women are all so different. They come from different backgrounds; their experiences and educations are not the same. Yet, the only thing that matters is they overcame the hesitation to show up, get support, and took action for what they want. They're showing up in ways they never had and feeling better than they ever believed possible. I can't wait for you to meet them.

More important, I can't wait for you to join them.

I have personally witnessed countless transformations of women who were just like me: in debt, wondering what their purpose was and what talents or influence they had. It's been one of the greatest joys of my life to see so many women starting businesses, using their influence to create positive change in others, becoming proven leaders, writing books, and speaking on stages, all while growing their personal knowledge and wallets.

IT MAY SEEM impossible now. You may be doing all you can to get what you want, only to be shackled by your limiting beliefs and fear-based stories. My journey started out the very same way, with a simple nudging that I was meant to be doing bigger things. I think that's how it starts for most of us! I wanted something more for myself. I couldn't quite put my finger on what that "more" might be at the time, but I knew that what I was doing wasn't working for me. I wanted to feel powerful, in control of my time and money—in short, I wanted *freedom*. I'm here to remind you to no longer underestimate the power of that small but mighty voice inside you that knows what she wants.

You picked up this book because you are or have been at the proverbial dining room table and you are sick and tired of being sick and tired. You're sick of being broke or in debt. You're sick of lying to yourself, your friends, or your loved ones. You're ready to shed the old beliefs, take action, and begin influencing others as well. For some of you, your goals might be to earn extra spending cash or buy a bigger house with a yard where you can grow that organic garden you've always wanted. For others it may be launching the multimillion-dollar company you've always dreamed of. Regardless of what your goal is, this book will help you discover what's holding you back and how you can move forward, so you can *Get What You Want*!

PART ONE

Realizing the Possibility

CHAPTER ONE

What's Holding You Back?

It's the first week of March 1999. All the privileged kids my age are about to find out if they have been accepted to the private school of their choice based on their expertise or vocation. Some are hoping to go the creative route, some the academic path, and some are hoping to play sports. Other kids, born into the right families, are choosing their schools based on where their parents went. They're counting on nepotistic favors.

None of these options were available to me. As a thirteen-year-old girl who grew up in a working-class small town, I had been thrust into this privileged world when, a few years prior, my mom moved us from our small town to Nashville, Tennessee, and then met my stepfather. Even though I had a couple years to get used to it, it was still a whole new world to me. From the outset, I struggled with feeling like an outsider. At the time I didn't know why, but my feelings of not belonging were undeniable. The other kids seemed to have gotten a memo that did not come to me. They all had the right hair, right clothes, and right attitude. I was a pudgy eighth grader with round glasses and thick, blunt bangs that made me look like a version of Daria Morgendorffer from the show *Daria*, minus the acerbic tone and combat boots. I didn't make honor roll, I wasn't a star athlete, and I didn't excel in music. Nor did I have the right last name. Creative, academic, sporty, and gifted were not adjectives that were used to describe me.

My stepdad generously poured his hard-earned money into this private middle school so that I could gain access to better education. He is a smart, vital, honest man of faith. As a prominent leader in the community who ran a successful business, he could afford to grant me access to things like private school and country clubs. And I know how lucky I am to have had him truly care. Of course, these were places that I knew nothing about from my small-town upbringing. I was invited to people's beach houses for spring break and over-the-top bat mitzvahs. I'd never seen anything like it. Where I was born and grew up for the better part of my childhood, no one had beach houses. No one had a TV in their car, theatre rooms, manicured lawns, or icemakers that made that awesome ice that I thought you could only get from Sonic. Where I'm from, no one even knew how to say or spell "bat mitzvah." After being introduced to all of this, my thirteen-year-old mind just started to expand with the idea that, *Ooh, wow! This is possible!* So I had all the hope in the world that I, too, would be invited to be part of the privileged group of high schoolers to be accepted to a private school. A small part of me was like, *Yeah, I belong here. Why not?* For the first time, I was beginning to understand that there was a world outside of my own. A world of limitless opportunity, abundance, money, and freedom. This was my first glimpse of seeing the way other people lived, worked, worshipped, communicated, and shared. Being able to witness what was possible was an incredible privilege, but it also came with a caveat.

Because of my own upbringing, all this wealth, success, abundance, and privilege made me feel like a fraud. Like I was living someone else's life. After all, this is not where I came from, and it wasn't what I was born into.

It was as though I was conditioned to believe in only what I had seen or known.

Back to that day in March 1999. I was in school waiting to hear the news. Was I accepted into the prestigious all-girls private school that was the natural next step for all the privileged girls at my middle school?

Every friend of mine that had applied was in. Their parents had called the school that day to let them know.

But for me? All I heard was crickets. Nada. Nothing.

I tried not to let my mind go to the worst-case scenario. Deep down I had a sense of dread, but I wouldn't allow myself to admit it. Instead, I placated myself for the rest of the day: *Of course, I was in. Of course, they wanted me. No one else seemed to be rejected.* I figured my mom wanted to wait to tell me in person so we could celebrate together.

When I got home that afternoon, I ran into the kitchen to grab a snack (my favorite hobby) and was met by my mom who had a very sad look on her face.

In that instant, I knew.

"They don't want me, do they?" I said, while I stuffed my face with Oreos, trying my best to numb the realization that what I had been fearing was true all along.

All I could think at that moment was: *My whole future is over. I'm not going to this great high school. I'm not going to go to college. Everything my mother has worked for and done was for naught.*

My mom, always trying her best to figure out the ideal solution to any situation, quickly perked up. "They've put you on the waiting list, but I've already spoken to them about getting you in soon! They clearly don't know what's good for them, and to be honest, I don't know how I feel about you even going to a school that could make such a stupid mistake like this! I mean, I thought they were supposed to be smart over there!"

My mom is a force to be reckoned with. She was born into a loving home with four siblings. Her dad, my grandfather, was the small-town realtor. Her mom, my grandmother, was a homemaker with an incredible gift of painting that was never fully realized. My mom never went to college, but she had enough street smarts and people skills to have earned a PhD in Life. She's a master at sales, persuasion, and getting what she wants while at the same time making people feel really good about the decision. "Make them think it's *their* idea," she'd always tell me. She's a *fake it 'til you make it* type and believes doing so taps into a divine source of power. She'd rather starve than take a handout, and always takes *no* as a jumping-off point to start negotiations. To put it simply, she was an influencer before being an influencer was cool. A lot of my relentlessness, determination, resourcefulness, and unwavering faith comes from her.

Looking back and being a mother now, I can only imagine how hard days like that were for her, though she never let me see it. She wanted so badly for her children to have a life that she knew was possible, but she could only control so much.

As my mom always says, you truly are only ever as happy as your least happy child.

The thing is, I was never waitlisted. My mom just told me that to make me feel better. The truth was I was flat-out denied. I never told my mom that I had overheard the real conversation she had on the phone with the school's administrator later that week. In her stern voice, she said, "You're telling me that you're not going to let her in? She is only one of two girls in her entire school that didn't get in. So you're going to break up two girls from their entire friend circle? From everything that they know? And that makes you feel good to accept an entire grade except for two girls?"

At that moment, all my negative beliefs started flooding my body. *I was right. I don't belong. They don't want you here. They would see through you sooner or later, you fake. Who do you think you are?*

I knew better than to think that I could truly be accepted as I was. I didn't have the grades, or the athletic ability, or the right last name. My biggest fear was coming true: the community that I so badly wanted to be a part of slammed the door on me and said, "No, thank you! Julie need not apply."

This experience led me to create an internal dialogue that I allowed to hold me back for years. The story was that I was an outsider. I didn't belong. I wasn't worthy.

This feeling of rejection stayed with me for decades. If it wasn't a school, it was a job, a guy, or a community I wanted to belong to. It was a pattern that would continue to repeat itself. Everywhere I went I wanted to belong. Every person I was with I wanted to love me just to validate my human existence. Validation is such a powerful, driving force in all of our lives. It's what compels us to do all sorts of things, like achieve.

Validation can be the difference between rising

out of the ashes or self-destructing completely.

What was also happening in this moment was an identity crisis. *Who am I anyway? Where do I belong?* We spend most of our lives trying on new masks to please other people, instead of focusing on what makes us feel whole and worthy. *Does this one fit? Do these people like me in this mask?* And then we get reaffirmed—or not. People accept us—or they don't. We just keep trying on masks until we find the one that works enough for most people to like us. This smile works, this attitude works, this body posture works, these clothes work, or this school or community works. But works for *whom?* For *them?* Of course, we get something out of it. We get affirmation and acceptance. But at what cost? One day we wake up and realize we're liked and affirmed for our masks, but not for our real, true, authentic selves. And worse, we start to have trouble keeping hold of what our authenticity looks like.

Like most girls in middle school, I was trying to figure out where I belonged and who I was. I was rejected from being who I thought I was becoming. I wasn't good enough just being Julie. Couple this with my own insecurity and feeling shame for not being born into this privileged world, and it was a recipe for some serious self-loathing. I knew I had to dig deep, start over, and build myself from the ground up.

Never did I want to come across as some weak victim. I would sometimes find myself thinking, *Oh, boohoo, Little Orphan Julie, you felt out of place at your little private school? Oh, I feel so bad for you because a great man married your mom and helped your parents support you. Get over yourself!*

But here's the real fact: It doesn't matter where you're from. It doesn't matter whether you're rich, poor, or anywhere in between. We all have shame. I have had no money, and I have had a lot of money, and I can attest both come with a heaping pile of shame. Having this mindset of growing up with not a lot of money and seeing how poverty-stricken my dad's upbringing had been, I was indoctrinated to believe that we didn't have enough.

Shame doesn't discriminate. The shame of not having enough feels just like the shame of having more than enough.

Most important, receiving without

shame is one of the most challenging

things I see many women face.

MY ORIGIN STORY

Do you know what an origin story is? In the DC and Marvel comic worlds, it's the detailed journey of how normal-seeming people end up saving the world all while having hot bodies.

There are usually tights involved, which is the only thing my origin story and the comic origin stories have in common. Instead of a superhero, though, I like to think of myself as a typical American girl, which sounds like either a kick-ass Tom Petty song or an overpriced doll that I begged my mom for as a child. I'm neither of those things, but I do have something in common with the doll: we each come with an emotionally satisfying backstory and more than a few jaunty accessories (each sold separately).

Also, somewhat like my story, those dolls start off their childhood encountering some massive life-changing event, like World War II, the Great Depression, or in the case of Samantha, growing up an orphan until her uncle adopts her and gives her a life of opportunity.

(By the way, this always seemed like a misstep to me. If you're introducing strong female characters to kids, perhaps you should start with a triumphant, non-bondage plotline? Where's that bra-less Gloria Steinem doll?)

Like Samantha, my origin story was not one of "in crowd" southern society and country club brunches. It was one of rejection and not belonging.

Growing up, I always needed everyone to like me. I distinctly remember in second grade throwing my beloved doll in the trash while crying my eyes out because a girl in my class said dolls were for babies and made fun of me. I adored that doll. With her long hair, big smile, and purple dress with matching purse, she had it all in my eyes. But having a classmate think less of me was worse than being honest about my love for my favorite Christmas gift. I was convinced she said what she said about my treasured doll because she didn't like me. I think it's because of that instinct that I always wanted to assimilate, blend in, look and talk like everyone else with the hope that people would like me. I also realized that anytime somebody liked me I automatically liked them back, only because they liked me. They saw something in me that was likable. I guess since I spent so much time and effort trying to be like everyone else, to blend in, that I had forgotten to find anything about myself that I liked.

And this story is one that owned me for many years.

I would see it thread through my life, like in my early thirties when I began to create what is now my business. I started to show up and support large groups of women by helping them create businesses they loved that made an impact, gained recognition, and saw success. Over time, tens of thousands of women joined my newsletter, invested in my programs, and listened to my podcast weekly to get the support they wanted. My origin story of not belonging began to change as I surrounded myself with like-minded women who shared my vision for greater success and freedom in their lives. Just when I thought I had gotten to the other side of my origin story, I came to realize that I hadn't dealt with some of the core beliefs around my lack of worthiness.

It was spring of 2017. I had recently launched *The Influencer Podcast,* and it was gaining real traction. I was putting a lot of time, love, and passion into the podcast: sourcing guests, interviewing them, writing blog posts, marketing content around the podcast, and engaging with the listeners on social media. I had thought about starting a podcast a few years prior, but due to lack of confidence and courage, I kept resisting. About six months prior to launching my podcast, another female entrepreneur had launched one. Witnessing the courage she had to get out there and make it happen was inspiring to me. I would listen to her podcast and hear the joy that it was bringing her, and the service it was providing to her community. In my eyes, she had it all: a top-rated podcast, a community of super loyal listeners, hundreds of thousands of followers on Instagram, and a beautiful visual brand. She was also the creator of successful online programs that were making her millions. She knew how to draw people in with her very real and raw content. She was one of the first people I saw sharing intimate parts of her personal life and was paving the way for beautiful conversations around body positivity and loving the skin you're in. Her content went viral, being liked and shared all over social media. She was known for her uplifting spirit, #communityovercompetition taglines, and being a girl's girl who helps other women reach their goals. On the outside looking in, her brand felt inspiring, motivating, and authentic. It was as though she had everything I aspired to have. I quickly put this woman on a pedestal. When I launched my podcast, I put her name, along with a few other women who had inspired me, in my podcast description as a nod of inspiration.

A few months after I launched my podcast, I had an episode titled "Want to Make $100K? Try This" that hit the top of the podcast episodes charts. It was all about business growth using my offer, prospect, sales method, and how to gain more followers and traction. Within a week the episode had been downloaded more times than any other episode in the same marketing category. The episode also took the #1 spot on the podcast marketing charts.

I was floored. Nothing like this had ever happened with any of the work I had done. And it felt good. It felt like I had finally landed on something that people wanted, and that I could provide. I felt like I finally found a place where I could belong, be seen, and shine.

The next week, to my surprise, an email from the woman whose podcast and business I had admired so much popped up in my inbox. I was so elated. I had no idea why she was emailing me, but I immediately went into fantasy mode. *Maybe she wants me to be on her podcast? Maybe she would come on mine? Maybe she wants to connect and be friends?*

Instead, I got this:

Huge congrats on launching your podcast, it looks great. We've never met but I just found your show on iTunes and noticed that you mention both my podcast name and my personal name in your description.

While I know you had pure (and wise) intentions, we were never approached about this or asked about it. As someone who's been working so hard at her podcast, I cringed a bit when I saw you riding the coattails of so many women who have done the same to help build your podcast up (without any relation, connection, or permission!).

I realize it's part of your strategy when it comes to people searching on iTunes but would it be possible to remove my information from your description as we or our sponsors aren't affiliated with your show?

I don't feel like it's a fair depiction of what you're doing and since I've never met you or been a guest on yours, I feel a little "off" about being listed right in your description.

I was frozen.

I remember staring at my computer. My jaw dropped and I felt a huge knot in my throat, while trying to hold back the tears. I couldn't believe my actions had made her *cringe*. I couldn't believe she thought I was trying to ride her coattails. That thought made me feel embarrassed and ashamed. The same story played through my head just as it had done when I was thirteen years old, and many times since. *They don't want you here. You don't belong. I knew they would see through you sooner or later, you fake. Who do you think you are?*

To say I was hurt and crushed would be an understatement. I couldn't believe that she had taken my inspiration that way. I was confused as I thought this woman, who had been such a leader in supporting other women and going after your goals, would have responded differently.

Part of me wanted to cry. Part of me wanted to call her out for not being who I told myself she was. Part of me wanted to write her back and say, "Oh, don't worry, I say far worse things to myself on a daily basis."

Instead, I got defensive. I felt like I needed to explain myself. I wrote her back trying to make her see my side and trying my best to show her we were relatable. My destructive people-pleasing patterns of trying to justify, rationalize, defend, and explain came roaring through as I desperately tried to show her that my intentions were pure. I wanted to prove to her that it never occurred to me that something so innocent as a praiseworthy mention needed approval from her or her team. I wanted her to understand. I wanted her to change her mind. I still wanted her to like me.

As much as I tried to force it, it still didn't work.

And here's the thing. She responded the way she did because people only see from their perspective and project from their own worlds. Her feelings were just as valid as mine. Yes, I was hurt, but it doesn't make her a bad person. Her response may have surprised me, but it also gave me an incredible gift: the gift to see people and things for what they really were, not for what I believed they were. It also taught me a profound lesson about self-love.

A woman who loves and trusts herself gives herself an incredible gift—the ability to love and trust other women.

I could now see how much I depended on the approval of people I looked up to and admired, and the effect it had on me. I felt like I was back in middle school waiting for the phone call that would change everything—that someone outside of me could validate my worthiness. And just like back when I was young, I believed I didn't belong. I believed in someone else's idea of me more than I believed in myself. I could finally wrap my head around how much this belief of needing to be accepted by others was holding me back, and the big part I had in it. I could finally see how all this desire to please was putting my own happiness in the hands of people I didn't even know.

This isn't just me. So many of the women I coach also struggle with this sense of belonging but still need the validation of others to give themselves the permission to belong.

Why is our own self-confidence, value, acceptance, and approval contingent on what other people think? The answer comes down to this: because it makes us feel better about not liking ourselves.

This comes from our origin story—the story we believe about ourselves. I believed I wasn't worthy unless someone invited me to their party, their school, their podcast, their "club"—their social media circle. I didn't feel like I belonged anywhere, and I desperately wanted to belong.

The problem with our origin story is that it holds us back.

We fall victim to our origin story when

we use it to define our current reality.

When triggered like that, we cease to grow. Our brains become fixed, finite, and self-limiting. We can't see other possibilities, which is the perfect opportunity for our excuses to come in and play a leading role in our lives. Our origin story becomes our excuse for everything we don't want to face in our own lives.

What's the payoff of living from your origin story? It usually is that you don't have to take personal accountability for your life. You can continue to play the victim, live inauthentically, and it's everyone else's fault. The payoff is that the problem remains "them" or "out there." The payoff is that your issues are for someone else to solve. The payoff is using perfectionism as the excuse to blame others for our own suffering. Perfectionism is just a tool that lets you blame everything going wrong in the world for your current situation.

Perfectionism is just a mask of victimhood.

The insidious thing about "blaming" others is we turn that blame inward eventually. We begin to believe we must be deeply flawed. We think we're unfixable, so again, what's the point? We are not good enough or smart enough to have solved this problem for ourselves. We think it was something we did or did not do.

These are our feelings of guilt and shame.

Nicole's Origin Story

I saw this coming up recently with a coaching client of mine. Nicole is a third-generation Latina who runs a marketing strategy company. On a recent coaching call, she shared with me that a big part of her always felt like she was attaching her worth and value to the success of her clients. She confided in me that she felt the most anxiety and frustration when she thought she was failing her clients. After all, their success is fundamentally tied to her success. The weight of tying her clients' outcomes to her success was becoming too much to bear. It was holding her back from her own success. I walked her through my steps on unlocking the root cause of the pain, which led to her origin story.

Nicole's origin story starts with her mom, who had Nicole when she was fifteen years old. Her mom came from an abusive household, as did Nicole's grandmother. Her grandmother was forced into prostitution to provide for her family and created a journey full of struggle and pain.

Nicole's mom was a high school dropout with little means. Fearful of not being able to provide the best kind of life for her child, she tried to abort Nicole multiple times. Then, in her eighth month she turned to a local healthcare clinic to get some help.

Watching her single mother struggle to survive created a belief system for Nicole. She came to believe there were limitations on abundance, success, and freedom. As Nicole grew up, went to college, and started her own company, she began to see success. But her unconscious beliefs caused her to self-sabotage opportunities.

Whether Nicole realized it or not, she was behaving this way because deep down she believed that in order to be successful in life, she had to struggle just like her mother and grandmother did before her.

These self-limiting beliefs made her feel less confident in the work she did. It made her want to disappear or resist launching new services, all of which had ramifications on her business.

"I feel like I can't put myself out there yet again," Nicole told me. "I can't share the wins or successes I am having, when I have clients who are paying me and aren't seeing that same kind of success I am seeing. It almost makes me feel like I give myself this excuse that I can't put myself out there."

Nicole saw this modeled in her own home, in the relationship between her mother and grandmother. Her mother felt shame for wanting more because her mom, Nicole's grandmother, had to struggle so much. It was as if Nicole's mom believed she needed to inherit the struggle in order to prove her love and loyalty to her family. And now Nicole was believing the same.

So I asked her, "Do you believe that you're a mirror for your clients?"

"I do," she said. "I don't know if that's good or bad."

And then I asked, "Do you think that if you are succeeding and you choose to share that with them and with the world, that maybe that would give them the permission they need to do the same? That instead of having them inherit your limiting belief, could they inherit your success? And I'm wondering if you're keeping yourself small to make your clients feel better? I wonder if that may be holding you back?"

It immediately clicked for Nicole. She was able to see how spot-on that new perspective was and how her origin story had been holding her back. I explained to Nicole that being on a different level than her customers is not a bad thing. That is the entire point of why they hired her. She is their leader. They are looking to her to lead. The more Nicole shines her light, the more she creates the path to shepherd her community along the path as well.

But if she chooses to let her origin story hold her back, there will be a lot of people out there who won't find her because the path is either too dark or not visible at all.

I said, "We know that you've tried dimming your light and watering down what you're happy about, what you're proud of, and what you've accomplished. You've done that, and we know how it makes you feel and the results that it gets you." Then I asked, "What else could you try?"

Nicole took a deep breath and with confidence said, "I could try just being completely unashamed of my successes. But it's so hard for me to talk about success without feeling shame or the concern that I'm rubbing someone the wrong way or coming across as bragging."

I stopped Nicole in that moment and asked her, "Well, what would happen if you rubbed someone the wrong way?"

She said, "That wouldn't matter to me, except from the perspective of if they were a client of mine." Then she paused. It was like a light bulb went off. "However, I don't really think any of my clients would think that way. I think that's just me. That's my fear of success."

I then asked, "Have you ever had a client say, 'I want to stop working with you because I think that you're bragging'?"

We both busted out laughing as Nicole said, "Definitely not!"

I asked her if she thought she could give herself permission to just shine brighter. She said she believed it was possible. It's this limiting belief around our origin story that made women like myself and my coaching clients like Nicole become such high achievers. The biggest motivator for high achievers is *I don't want people to see me as anything less.* So that relentlessness to achieve can bring successes. It's helped me help women just like Nicole, but it can also hold us back if we aren't mindful of how we're using it.

Fast-forward to today. Nicole no longer believes in the origin story that held her back for so many years. Nicole was able to shed her old stories and set new heights for herself that year, bringing in over six figures in revenue, more than she had ever done. She also saw her mom release limiting beliefs as well. Nicole's mom is now the COO of the very same healthcare clinic that helped her give birth to Nicole years ago. So it's a beautiful, full-circle story of perseverance. There's an incredible amount of redemption in their family unit as well. Her mom went through a healing process with her grandmother. Nicole has been able to witness this continued progression within her family legacy. Nicole is a great example of what can happen when we release the bond of our origin story, and no longer let it hold us back. We not only have the power to transform ourselves, but we have the power to transform and heal others as well.

If hurt people can hurt people,

healed people can heal people.

Your Origin Story

What is your origin story? We all have one. It may be around relationships, money, achievement, success. The list goes on.

- What is it that's holding you back?
- Where do you feel like you don't belong?

- Where do you feel unworthy and helpless?
- What ways are you resistant to receive support and why?

All the decisions that we make—whether in our business, our home, or our relationships—come from a core belief that is born out of our origin story.

Whatever that core belief is, that's what we're going to live out. For example, if you learned as a child that you can't trust anyone or that someone is always out to get you, then it's going to come into play when you become an adult and start to work and live your life, because you carry that belief with you. This is how your origin story has an impact on how you live your life and show up in the world.

Just because you've always believed something to be true doesn't mean that it is true. You might not be able to change how you were raised, but you can change how you believe that story. You can change your beliefs.

If you want to change, you need to change the way you think about yourself and the world around you.

You get to change. You get to disrupt. You get to make different choices.

Sometimes we don't feel like we can because we are worried what our family will think of us. Or what our friends, neighbors, heck, even strangers on Instagram will think of us. Consider this your permission slip to change. Consider this your invitation to a whole new group where you will always belong. It's a group of people who aren't willing to let others hold them back. You're welcome here. I'm here. We're all here waiting for you. Join us.

Doing the Work

This work is key to helping you identify your origin story. If you want to be able to move on in the chapters ahead where you identify what you want (and not just doing what you think you should) you need to get to the bottom of your origin story and deal with it once and for all. Own your story, because when you reject parts of it, you give others the permission to reject you too!

THE 3A'S

Because I had spent years paving a path to unworthiness, I knew I could also pave a path out. I had to do the footwork down a new pathway, and that started with three things: awareness, acceptance, and action. They are known as the 3A's in twelve-step literature and therapy circles. Before I could embrace my worthiness, I had to accept my origin story. Before acceptance, I had to become aware. Before awareness, I had to be brutally honest with myself. This took work. It's from this work that I created my own toolkit and unlocked the control my origin story had over me.

UNLOCKING YOUR ORIGIN STORY WITH THE 3A'S

I run through the 3A's with any challenge that comes my way until I get the answers that will move me forward. Why? Because small actions bring clarity, which makes us feel better. In feeling

better, we are clearer about what we can do to effect the bigger changes we want.

Whenever you start anything new, whether it's a business or diving into a passion, you will be confronted daily with origin stories, like impostor syndrome, not feeling good enough, and perfectionism. You will be praising yourself at breakfast and second-guessing yourself by lunchtime.

Remember the letter I received from the podcaster I put on a pedestal? If I were to have gotten that letter today, I wouldn't feel the need to defend myself. I just wouldn't respond to an email like that. I would go about my life and do what felt right for me. Because I now know who I am and am secure in that. Nothing she could say would change the security and love I have for myself. Because now I know that my origin story no longer has control over me. It just doesn't hit the same way. Thanks to the tools I'm about to introduce, I no longer put myself in a position where I feel that my value is contingent on somebody else.

Your origin stories will always come up.

And, unless you can deal with them,

you aren't going to go to the next level.

They will just keep dragging you back.

Awareness

Awareness is always the first step in any recovery process. Recovering from your origin story is no different. This is about understanding where you are, where you are heading, and where you want to go. You need the facts. This is eye-opening fact-finding. This is listening to what is really happening inside of your mind and body, getting past false assumptions, letting go of denial, facing the hard truth, and grasping the reality of what is holding you back. This is more difficult than you imagine because you don't know what you don't know. The barrier of denial is invisible until you crash right through it.

Understanding the old stories you tell yourself is crucial. This will help you start to notice the destructive belief patterns you've been loyal to. Most of us are not even aware of the nature of what's holding us back, or of its impact on us. Also, we may see the problems in our lives and yet fail to recognize our origin story as the source.

Ironically, because our entire lives are wrapped up in our origin story, we fail to notice its everyday presence holding us back, like gravity trying to pull you down when you take off in an airplane. Survival skills can also change the way we remember our origin story. We hide our real feelings in order to survive, only to forget we ever had feelings in the first place. We adapt by believing the parts of our reality that suit us and ignore the rest. Then, we are devastated that reality didn't change after we chose to stick our heads in the sand. We lie, make excuses, belittle, and even rationalize our own faults and limitations to honor our origin story.

To feel safe, we may make the mistake of letting our deepest desires slip away from us. The result it that we may wind up as nothing more than a sad, vacant version of our true selves.

With awareness, we come to see how much energy we previously spent on escaping, ignoring, fleeing, and denying. Awareness comes up in many forms. Where is it in your body? My awareness always shows up in my throat. I know I am giving in to my origin story when that huge tennis ball emerges, which makes it hard for me to speak or even swallow. This is always my first sign that there is something I need to pay attention to. Thanks to awareness, I don't have to wait for a situation to explode before I face it.

How? Well, for me, a good mirror helps. I look for people who can be good role models for me, who can give me feedback, who can be honest with me when I head in a direction that takes me away from my true self. I look for other women and leaders who know how to cope with grace, who have a knack for quick problem solving, who are patient with themselves, and who know how to navigate the realities of life.

Second, I choose to start facing some harsh realities. Taking a moment to journal out my resentment, fears, and my part to play in both gets me face-to-face with those realities faster than anything else. We cannot see that we play a crucial role in creating our misery until we can finally face the reality that can keep us frozen for years, even decades. I recommend you do the same.

The benefit of awareness is that it thaws us out. Less frozen, we can be open to understanding the truth about a situation. We can take a whole new view of events and of our feelings about them.

Because here's the truth: life is a package deal.

It isn't enough to look only at the parts we like.

We must face the whole picture so that we

can make realistic choices and stop setting

ourselves up for disappointment.

We can't cope with something unless we acknowledge its reality. That's when movement can take place. With this movement comes freedom. Our reality no longer traps us.

Awareness gives us a beautiful gift: the ability to see things as they are. The truth is that we are worthy of love and joy, and we have so much to offer the world. Finding the parts we love and honor about ourselves takes time, but we begin the journey to freedom with acceptance. Living is more than mere survival. We are here because we are ready to heal from what holds us back. We are ready to see ourselves and our life in a new light. We are ready to be seen and loved for who we are, and awareness is our guide.

Acceptance

Acceptance is one of the most important steps in shedding your origin story. It's the step after awareness and before setting out in a new direction.

Acceptance is something that I must grasp again and again. I don't want to fail, and I don't want to be set up to fail. With acceptance, I can now adjust my expectations based on the reality of my situation and how circumstances beyond my control affect my ability to succeed. Expectations are nothing more than premeditated resentments. Acceptance allows me to lessen the blow of the expectations I place on myself and others.

With acceptance, we can have a good day regardless of other people's choices because we know our day depends on our own capacity to accept what is, exactly as it is.

How often is it that someone or something is unacceptable to us? You don't get the job, you hate your house, your spouse doesn't pay attention to you, you can't seem to make enough money, the community you lived in growing up sucked, nothing is working in your favor. All these circumstances and the expectations we place on them make up how we choose to be, think, and act each and every day.

Acceptance can go two ways. We either negatively accept or positively accept what is happening to us. When we live from our origin story, we self-destructively accept that we must endure toxic behaviors like abuse, disrespect, being controlled, or being treated poorly. Our origin story can tell us we deserve to be overlooked, unappreciated, or ignored. We think we have no choice but to let others use, manipulate, and not allow us to have a positive impact on our world. We also think we don't deserve love and validation, since our origin story didn't show us this.

Our origin stories are deeply ingrained. So much so that even when we begin to receive useful, valid new information about ourselves and the people in our lives (awareness), we still want to skip over the acceptance part. This also has to do with our origin story.

We may hesitate to accept an unpleasant reality because we see it as condoning behavior that we don't stand for, which just leads to more suffering. We also believe that we need to be "doing" all the time thanks to culture, in which our origin story is affected. Our culture values immediate gratification, not process. When we've been waiting so long for something or someone better to come along, we don't want it to take time. Our origin story has convinced us that if we're told to wait, it means it'll never happen, and we'll never get our needs met.

Our version of acceptance is painful and debilitating, so we keep trying to ignore it altogether, as if we could control the truth away! The way out of this is radical acceptance, acknowledging the truth about things, without any expectation or mask. It's only about what is or was. Not what we wish things were, what we think they should be, what others say things are, or even what could potentially be. Acceptance doesn't mean we submit to a degrading situation. It means that we accept the facts, then decide what to do about it.

Radical acceptance means that we have neither the power nor the right to change others, and that it is our responsibility to see and accept people as they really are, not ignoring the parts that hurt us. It requires that we slowly let go of all our baggage, dropping the rags of our origin story, piece by piece, as if it were an old baby blanket that was ready to be laid to rest. Only then can we patiently move our true selves into a beautiful new space that feels healthy, aligned, honest, and integral.

Bottom line: you will not get what you want until you accept that person, place, thing, or situation as being exactly the way it is, and nothing more.

Acceptance allows us to rise above what we once considered impossible. As soon as we accept our limitations, we open the door to endless possibilities. We may have to relearn what it means to be accountable. Accountable for our own thoughts, feelings, actions, reactions, and results.

Acceptance also snaps us back to reality. Acceptance allows us to let go of the illusion that holds us back and to discover the freedom and power we have to define our lives the way we want. Acceptance always reminds me of the Serenity Prayer, historically attributed to the American theologian Reinhold Niebuhr. "God, grant me the serenity to accept the things I cannot change, the courage to change the things I can, and the wisdom to know the difference."

Action

Action is taking the steps to get where we want to go. Once we are aware of our destination and have accepted where we are today, we are ready to go! All we need is a vehicle. That vehicle is called choice, and it's going to be more like a motorcycle with one of those side seats. We will be exposed to the elements of the real world. At times it will be uncomfortable, but quite exhilarating, rather like a roller-coaster ride.

With action, you get to decide: Do you want to be right, or do you want to be happy? Because sometimes, we can't have both. And that doesn't give us a free pass not to act. Not acting is what has held us back long enough, so now you have a choice. You get to have the agency to decide who you want to be at the end of this to get what you want. And the best part? You now have awareness and acceptance in your toolbox. You get to ask yourselves questions like, "How important is it?" on your road to action, which gives you the perspective you need. If we take the time to think about what really matters, each of us is free to determine for ourselves what is truly worth our time and energy. Is our husband forgetting to load the dishwasher worth the cost of our happiness? What price are you willing to pay to win an argument or to prove to other people that you are right? Does it really matter? Must we take it all so personally? Even if we decide that the situation is important, we can ask ourselves whether it is important today.

Today is all we have. Why waste this precious gift of time on trivial concerns when we could be taking action? Taking action means we have to "just do it" even if we can't control or predict what happens next. We need to speak our truth, finish projects, gather groups, rouse the community, enable our own faculty to lead, and always remain teachable.

Action means you're doing yourself

a massive favor. You no longer leave

five minutes before the miracle happens.

YOUR TURN

Awareness

Write your origin story. What is the story you tell yourself why you can't do something? What triggers you? Sometimes you must dig deep and go back to an early memory like I did. No one is judging you. Don't hold back.

_____

_____

_____

Acceptance

Has there been something about yourself, someone else, or a situation that you have not been willing to accept? If so, what outcomes are you getting right now?

_____

_____

_____

What parts of yourself are you willing to finally accept? What can you change? What can you not change?

_____

_____

_____

Action

When thinking about what is holding you back, can you name what your part is? How are you going to go about changing it?

_____

_____

_____

Now you have a formula that you can use all the time, not just when it comes to your origin story. You can use the formula throughout your day and let it guide you. Here is how I have found it works well. The 3A's turn into three statements to complete:

I am aware that _____.

I accept that _____.

My action is to _____.

You don't have to overthink your answers. They could look like these examples:

I am aware that I do enjoy the work I do, and that I am tired.

I accept that I don't feel like showing up for my meeting today.

My action is to take a walk before my meeting and go easy on myself during the meeting.

Or:

I am aware that there is risk to this, and also reward.

I accept that I am feeling nervous about leaving my corporate job and going all in on my entrepreneurial dreams.

My action is to repeat this exercise for more clarity. I know more will be revealed at the right and perfect time.

Or:

I am aware that I have some really good friends.

I accept that I am feeling scared and alone.

My action is to call a friend who has offered to help me.

Or:

I am aware that I cannot change my mother.

I accept that my mother is late whenever we arrange a time to get together.

My action is to take a book with me to read while I wait for her to join me.

CHAPTER TWO

What Do You Want?

In the summer of 2007, I graduated from college and moved to New York City. I had never been to New York except for one time a few months prior on a university journalism trip. I had fallen in love with the vibrance and possibility of the city and knew that was where I wanted to be. I moved to New York with no job, no place to live, and no friends. Through friends of friends, I was able to couch surf for a few months while I looked for a job. After about three months of tirelessly searching for a job and putting out resumes, I landed a position as a PR assistant for a music publicity agency. This agency was boutique and had an incredible reputation of working with some of the biggest and best music acts at the time. It was run by a fabulous woman who was a force to be reckoned with. She was powerful, independent, successful, and a bit scary. I had never met anyone like her before, nor did I see any of her strong qualities in myself.

The new city and new job brought with it my first taste of a culture and experience that I had never been a part of before. It was also my first time witnessing, daily, powerful women living their purpose and leading their path. These women were respected and admired for their work and abilities, not just for the way that they looked or acted.

My time in New York was life changing and challenging. As a PR assistant, I was expected to survive on $25,000 a year in one of the most expensive cities in the world. In addition to the $3,000-a-month, one-bedroom apartment that I converted into a two-bedroom so I could split the high rent with someone, I owed $30,000 in school loans. Fortunately for me, my mom and stepdad generously decided to help ease the strain on my wallet by giving me $500 a month to put toward my rent. (This only covered about 35 percent of what I owed but was still a tremendous help.) Nevertheless, I had to make every dollar count in order to take care of my basic needs. Then there was also the added pressure that I had to eventually make it on my own.

My mom made it clear that this help was just temporary. "Look, we can help you for about twelve months with this," she said. "Then you are on your own."

I ALWAYS SAY that I learned more in one year in New York than most people learn in a decade there. It was fast and tough. I was thrown into the fire more than once but what I got to experience was the gift of seeing, for the first time ever, strong women of different colors, races, beliefs, and backgrounds not only leading an industry, but damn near owning it. The owner of the company, Linda, took no prisoners. My boss, Carlene, was an incredible mentor. I learned from this experience what it meant to ask for what you want, how to negotiate for what you deserve, how to influence others to get on board with your ideas, and most important, how to achieve remarkable results. But as clear as I was that I wanted to be here, I was running out of money. I might have learned how to "ask for what you want," but I had yet to figure out how to make that work for myself.

Weeks turned into months. After more than a year with no raise in sight, I knew deep down I could no longer go on financially without the support of my parents, let alone without the tools and life skills to figure out my next steps. The only thing that I knew to do was to go back to what was safe.

I made an appointment with Linda and Carlene to put in my two weeks' notice. As I sat in her office and told her I couldn't afford to be there anymore, Linda asked how much it would cost for me to stay. I was so confused by that question. *How much?* I didn't know the opportunity to stay was possible so I couldn't give her an answer. I had no idea. I hadn't even considered it. I thought, *What does she mean? How much would it cost?* Looking back now, I know what she meant. She was giving me an opportunity to pitch myself, to negotiate for myself the way I had learned to do for our clients. To ask for and get what I wanted.

She was seeing me in a way that I had never seen myself. I had, up until that point in time, seen myself as a helpless person who always did and acted as everyone else did—who was making her way in the big city, but who also didn't think she could make it on her own. I was being called back to what was comfortable. In Tennessee I had a home, my family, my ex-husband who was my boyfriend at the time, and it felt as if they were all egging me to come back. But in New York I had women I admired saying they wanted me there. Saying that I had a place and belonged. This was my chance to become who I wanted to be, but I just couldn't see in myself what they saw in me, and it felt selfish to ignore the calls to come home.

Linda and Carlene believed in me, in a different way than other women had believed in me before. No teacher or coach had ever believed in me the way she did. Linda believed in my work, my ability to serve, and my ability to carry out a purpose. And that was what was so gut wrenching to me: I knew in that moment that I was giving up on my dream to be bigger and shine brighter, to work with amazing people, to do amazing things, without trying to fight for the future that I wanted for myself—the future I was fully capable of creating.

RETURNING HOME, I had mixed feelings of relief and shame. I was relieved not to be letting anyone down, but I was filled with shame, especially for not using my voice and for giving up on my dreams. But this experience taught me the most important lesson of all during my time in New York. The moment I told my bosses that I needed to go home, I knew I never, ever wanted to feel that way again. I never wanted to give up on my dreams again. I never again wanted money to be a determining factor in why I should have to give something up. I would never again sacrifice myself over money.

When I got back home to Tennessee, I fell into a mild depression. I felt lost, with no vision, passion, or purpose. I didn't know what my dream was, but I knew how that experience in New York made me feel. I just didn't know how to get back to that feeling. So I spent the next few years trying to figure out where I fit in the world. I transitioned my work from music PR to book PR and started to learn even more about the craft that would lay the foundation for the career I would have a decade later. I started to gain more corporate experience and wins. I was learning things, going to important meetings, sitting in on important discussions, and getting to work with some incredible authors.

Yet I was always searching for more. I spent several years trying to get back to that sense of feeling invigorated. I longed for feeling like what I was doing really mattered and brought joy to my life instead of just a time clock and a paycheck. The truth was, I didn't. I felt empty, and I knew I wasn't doing what I really wanted.

I got so consumed by caring about what other people thought and pleasing everybody else that I didn't even know how to give myself permission to know my own feelings. I had totally lost touch with what I, Julie, truly felt.

People-pleasing in order to connect with others

is like chewing gum to satisfy your hunger.

You crave true connection, but you only show people a cheerful, agreeable version of you. They like this version, even love it—but no matter how many compliments you get, you're still starving in the end. The obsession with people-pleasing turned me into a version of Jekyll and Hyde. I would either be a doormat that you could walk all over, or my frustration of pleasing would evolve into me becoming a self-righteous punisher hell-bent on making sure you knew how wrong you were for making me abandon myself.

I always felt that "there's got to be more than this." I had this vision, and I was so afraid to speak it out loud, afraid people in my life would suffocate the vision out of their own fear and protection of me.

It is an extremely vulnerable thing to share your vision with someone. Because doing so opens you up to false confirmations that you aren't good enough for the vision, which is the biggest fear of all. My family thought I was crazy. They would say to me, "Julie, you're never satisfied, what is wrong with you?" My ex-husband would get dismissive; he didn't understand why I didn't feel content or happy. He would always tell me I was like a unicorn that could never be caught.

When you hear from people all the time, "When are you going to be satisfied?" you start to believe that something is wrong with you. But in fact, they're asking the wrong question. Whatever happened to questions like:

"What lights you up?"

"What do you enjoy doing that also feels really good?"

"What brings you the most joy?"

At the time I didn't have the answers to those questions. I just knew that I did not want to be sitting in that dark cubicle anymore.

BUT HERE IS the million-dollar question that I was afraid to ask myself: *What do I really want?* I wanted to see the world, but I was told I couldn't. I wanted to feel safe, but many times I didn't. I so badly wanted to be loved and seen but was afraid that people would see the real me. What if they didn't like me? What if they left? Then I'd be alone. As a child I learned to walk on eggshells and not make waves. If I was perfect, everything would be fine. But when I became so focused on making others feel good, I totally lost sense of what made me feel good. How in the world could I find that out? How could I self-actualize and find joy and purpose if I was so busy just trying to be safe, just trying to get by? And the things happening in my professional life were being mirrored in my relationship with my ex-husband.

After seven years of being off and on in our relationship, we had given each other a "shit or get off the pot" ultimatum. We were either moving forward together or not. (I know, totally romantic. The stuff dreams are made of, right?)

The night my ex-husband and I met, we spent the evening staying up all night at a party. It wasn't during some wild evening like you would see in the movies. It was just the two of us, fawning over each other's attempts to feel like we belonged.

Now it may shock some of my clients and followers that I was part of the wild crowd. In the social circles I was in, drinking and recreational drugs were the norm. But I felt it was important to share this and show you just how willing I was to go along with the crowd. I did my fair share of experimenting, but recreational drugs were never really my thing. However, it was the drug of choice of many of the people that I loved being around. And my drug of choice were those people. You know, the ones you think need you to save them from themselves? Being the hero in everyone else's story: that was my addiction.

The complex people who lived with more reckless abandon were always the most interesting to me. And even though I would be the friend at the party who would be falling asleep on the couch at 4:00 a.m. while everyone raged on (this literally happened on more than one occasion), it all felt normal and comfortable to me. We will always pick the comfortable or familiar over what is best for us. Always. My relationships were passionate, chaotic, and unpredictable. I knew this growing up, and this is what I was drawn to as an adult.

You see, that's the thing with people-pleasing,

I lied so well that I even convinced myself!

Nevertheless, I was what you might call a high-functioning codependent—responsible in college and very clear about my plans. I had learned throughout my childhood how praised I was for being a good chameleon. The terror of being found out was always greater than the fear of not being loved for who I was. So, I adapted.

All of this is okay. Everything is completely normal and fine! See how good I am at school and partying? I fit in everywhere!

Who am I? *I am whoever you want me to be, and more!* Of course, the biggest hurdle I was left with was that I had conned myself. My fear of looking bad or feeling less than was my driving force in how I showed up in life and in all relationships. And this fear kept me shaping myself into whomever and whatever I needed to be to make everyone adore me.

You see, at this time in my life I had always been a different person to different people. Lackluster to one. Talented to another. Inviting to most and isolating to a few. Popular to some and unknown to a lot. Of course, this was all a defense mechanism, keeping me safe from rejection and abandonment. I stayed with my ex-husband for as long as I did because he was my security blanket. He was my comfortable companion. Even when we would break up and I would run off to try and save some other guy, I would always come running back to him. He was what I told myself was safe, right, stable. And in a lot of ways, he was. My family said to me, "No one is ever going to love you as much as he does. He will never leave you, abandon you, or cheat on you. You don't have to worry about him. He's not crazy. He's not a bum. He's not an addict. What's wrong with you?" Well, what was wrong was that I was so codependently entangled with him. I didn't even know how to be my own person. I would always abandon myself by overcommitting, over-functioning, worrying, stressing myself out trying to fix things, and controlling things to avoid the distress caused by my own inability to speak the truth. I was so afraid of being alone that I would do whatever was necessary not to be alone.

And that's the thing with codependency. We think we live in a world of just ourselves where everybody else is playing a part. We forget there's another person who has wants, needs, dreams, and desires. They may also be scared to ask for what they truly want, because they are also codependent and scared of loss. My ex-husband and I kept each other from living our best possible lives, because we were so caught up in trying to stay safe.

I needed him to be okay in order to feel okay too. And the only way I thought he would be okay was if we got married and I never left him. If I never told him my big dreams and goals, if I never shared with him how rich and full a life I wanted to be, then he wouldn't be scared away and all could stay as it was: familiar, safe, comfortable, small.

I married the first man I ever loved and told myself that this is what love is, sacrificing myself for our marriage. It hurt to feel anything because feelings were only a reminder of the joy I thought I no longer deserved. So, I shut my feelings off like flicking a switch, by repeating a little mantra of "It's fine, I'll figure it out." After a few repetitions, I'd go numb. That was my pattern. That was how I managed to stay with my ex for seven years, by using the same techniques learned earlier in life, by numbing myself from the truth. And this pattern taught me one of the most profound lessons in my life . . .

You can't hide yourself and expect to be seen.

Numbing myself stunted my ability to experience joy, delight, and fulfillment. This is another one of those blasted either/or truths: we get none of the feelings, or all of them. Pain and sorrow are included in the package. If I want the joy and the delight, I must accept the full scope of my feelings. You cannot separate love from heartbreak, shame from empathy, joy from grief.

That means in order to get what you want, you must be all in! It's part of the universal contract we all make by deciding to live a full life. As author and podcast host Brené Brown says, "The brokenhearted are the bravest among us. They dared to love." You must decide for yourself how fully engaged you want to be in your own life experience.

After years of trying to make it work, I decided to end the marriage. I kept looking in the mirror, trying to recognize the person there, until it became too unbearable to deny. I could no longer go another day without listening to my gut, and most important, act upon it. I chose to end my marriage because my heart was finally ready for the woman I always knew I could be when I decided to love myself more than any man.

My biggest regret with my first husband is that I confused pity with love and caring with control, because I didn't know how to give him the simple dignity of being himself.

So how could I truly love and respect him? It's when we choose to love others without losing ourselves that we learn to accept love in return.

PEOPLE WHO SPEND their lives pleasing others never find the truth. They never find what they want, because they spend their whole life pleasing. Pleasing their mother, pleasing their father, pleasing their spouses or their friends or their bosses. When you spend your entire life walking on eggshells, you can't be who you need to be because you must make everybody else happy and peaceful.

I didn't know what I wanted, but I was starting to articulate very clearly what I didn't want. I started to see that I could be a good person with a kind heart and still say, "No, this isn't for me." Knowing what I didn't want helped me create that path to what I did want, even though I had these feelings of shame, remorse, and regret. And I think that is one of the hardest parts of getting what we want: saying it out loud and coming clean to those in your life. For me, this began with creating boundaries for the first time in my life.

THE IMPORTANCE OF BOUNDARIES

In my first marriage I had no explicit boundaries. On a subconscious level I always had a sense of what was and was not acceptable to me, but I didn't feel entitled to act on those feelings. Instead, I would grow resentful, frustrated, and angry whenever those hidden boundaries were crossed. *I know I don't care enough about my own needs to speak up for them, but how dare someone not read my mind and care enough to meet my needs and respect my boundaries! Shame on them!* I felt like a helpless victim and spent many long hours with the poor-me's.

My lack of boundaries also left me confused. I was so focused on him that I could not see where he left off and I began. I lost my sense of what was appropriate and okay. How can we distinguish between acceptable and unacceptable behavior when we don't even know what we want or need?

My first marriage taught me the difference between walls and boundaries. Walls are solid and rigid. They keep others out. They kept me trapped inside. Boundaries are flexible, changeable, and removable. It's up to me how open or closed I'll be at any given time. Boundaries let me decide what behavior is acceptable, not only from others but from myself.

Knowing my boundaries does not mean forcing others to change; it means that I know my own limits and take care of myself by respecting them.

The focus today, and every day, is finally on me. Today I have the option to set limits, to draw a line that I will not allow to be crossed. I may not please everyone, but in the long run I think that is a more open and honest approach.

The way I know I'm living within healthy boundaries today is when I no longer delay my happiness, and I don't subject myself to the judgments or abuse of other people.

There's something magical about reaching that point of becoming ready to settle into your boundaries with confidence, which I detail in the next chapter. We know what we mean, we mean what we say, and others take us seriously too. Things change, not because we're controlling others, but because we changed.

The hardest part of setting and sticking to my boundaries has been to do this with love. It is so easy for me to justify my decisions by blaming other people and making them the villains so that I won't feel so guilty. But there is no villain. Blaming, judging, and justifying only harm an already fragile relationship. I don't ever want to forget that I am capable of love. I believe that it is far more loving to allow others the dignity of facing the consequences of their actions without interference from me. Newsflash: I do not have to be everyone's savior. I'm not the Giving Tree! I do not have to have all the answers. I do not have to figure it all out. What a freaking relief!

This was not an easy decision for me to make, and I have paid a price. I had to give up my tremendous need to control what happens to other people. I have been forced to place my faith and trust in believing that I do not know what's best for everyone around me.

Since that time, we have both moved on. My ex-husband is now happily married with a family, as am I. Today, I have a life of my own. I have work that I love, hobbies, good friends, a growing relationship with my husband, and a business that continues to thrive. My life is far from perfect, and things still bother me. It's hard not to want to try to control, manipulate, and manage my way through so much in my life. But thanks to boundaries, it is no longer the single most important issue. I now get to focus on healing. I now get to fall in love with me.

Thanks to boundaries,

I will learn truths about myself and

have the confidence to stand by them.

As we heal, it's natural to grieve for our younger selves who were unable to set boundaries and protect their own bodies, minds, and hearts. Yes, you can survive the discomfort of setting a boundary. And the payoff is that you might just start to thrive. I shudder to think what Julie would have become had she gotten what she thought she needed in order to please others. Even worse, I shudder to think of all the things I would have missed out on: the deep and soulful connection with myself, my husband, and the birth of my two children, not to mention the career that wakes me up in the morning with feelings of gratitude, joy, and fulfillment. I think of all the people I wouldn't have been able to serve and help had I not helped myself, had I not had the courage to ask myself: *What do you want?*

CHAPTER THREE

Steps to Getting What You Really Want

I remember one of the first times I set a new boundary that changed my marriage. It was a summer day in May. I had rented a beach house in Malibu and invited friends for a BBQ to celebrate a recent business launch. Renting a beach house for the weekend was something I wanted to do for years but would always find a way to stop myself with the usual excuses. "It's expensive," I'd whisper to myself. "My husband won't care to spend our money and time this way." Before I created boundaries, I would use my origin story beliefs of manipulation, coercion, or omission to force whatever I wanted because I was terrified of being rejected, or worse, feeling disapproval for sharing what I wanted and desired. This time was set up to be no different.

To avoid the sting of rejection, I would create these situations that caused unnecessary chaos and drama.

First, I would drop subtle hints about my desire for a beach day gathering to my husband, hoping my charm would persuade him to get on board with the idea. If that didn't work, I would play another role: the damsel in distress. Acting like a sad and helpless toddler, hoping I could make him pity me enough to comply with my wishes. And finally, if nothing else prevailed, I would play the role of my lifetime, which consisted of doing whatever the hell I wanted to do and then telling him about it later if I felt like it. At that point, he'd have no choice but to live with the decision I made. I'm sure you can imagine how these situations would end—arguments that led to resentment and bitterness.

And yes, I am fully aware of how gross this behavior is. I am also fully aware that you're probably nodding to yourself right now because you or someone you know has done the exact same thing.

When you have no boundaries, you don't know how to communicate without feeling the need to rationalize or justify your feelings. You don't know how to say what you mean, mean what you say, and not say it mean.

Luckily, on this day, I chose to try something new. Instead of playing a role, I would create a boundary. One that Brené Brown would call "clear is kind." I was going to clearly and kindly share what I wanted, with no strings attached. Then, I would honor my boundaries by committing to my decision regardless of *his* response.

I told my husband, "I've rented a beach house in Malibu for the weekend and invited our friends. This is something I am excited about. It means a lot to me to celebrate in this way, and I'd love for you to join us. But if you can't or don't want to, that's okay too. I will still go and enjoy myself."

To which he replied, "Sounds good, count me in."

Although this may sound trivial and insignificant, it affected me profoundly. I had spent years dress-rehearsing chaos—which would create a chaotic situation—instead of just speaking what was on my heart and mind. But this seemingly minor exchange showed me that I could say what I mean, mean what I say, and not say it in a mean way. And that boundary, in and of itself, could get me what I want. The boundary does not mean that it will go my way. It means I give myself permission to be seen and heard as my whole, imperfect self.

I was starting to realize that I didn't have to protect myself from my husband's responses and reactions by building walls or causing chaos. I didn't have to delay my happiness at all. I just needed to create boundaries and honor them.

CREATING YOUR BOUNDARIES

Creating boundaries is not what people seem to think it is—putting up a wall around oneself so others can't penetrate it, or forcing what you want at the expense of your own honesty. A wall is built out of fear and mistrust. It blocks people and experiences out. Boundaries, on the other hand, are markers, low fences. People and experiences can come and go, but you are the guardian of who swings open that gate and what comes in. Boundaries help us reclaim our own lives. Boundaries help us define what we want in our space, and what we don't want. And we can't know what belongs there if we don't know ourselves in the first place. If we want to establish clear boundaries, we need to focus on ourselves, build our own strength, and ask for and accept help when we need it.

Often, people find it difficult to create boundaries because we have lost track of the separation between ourselves and others. I know this challenge intimately, having advocated for so long on the behalf of others in my lifetime. I spent years constantly reacting, worrying, pleasing, fixing, problem solving, and taking on responsibilities that didn't have my name on them. The result was that I lost the sense of where I left off and others began. After becoming so entangled in someone else's life and problems, I lost sight of the fact that we were separate people.

You're allowed to change the price

of what it costs to access you,

and boundaries are the currency.

It only made sense to me to respond, fix, and find solutions for everyone around me.

I also confused this absence of boundaries with love and caring. I became so fixated on the choices and decisions other people made, I would lose the ability to distinguish between myself and them.

This is not love—it's obsession.

By focusing on the lives of others instead of living our own lives, we move away from love and turn toward fear. Not only is it harmful to a relationship, it's also extremely self-destructive.

Another thing that can happen when we lack boundaries is that we delay our own happiness. I did this for years because I didn't want to upset the other person. I would act like I didn't care; I would tell myself that the self-sacrifice was for the sake of making them feel better. Honestly, it was an effort to feel that I had some power over them.

If you offer help or guidance more than

once, you're trying to control.

The choice to abandon our own happiness for such a purpose is an act of fear, not love. Boundaries allow us to move away from self-abandonment and toward self-love. True, healthy love isn't destructive or controlling. It doesn't diminish or strip us of our identities, nor does it in any way diminish those whom we love. Love is nourishing; it allows each of us to be more fully ourselves. Most important, it allows us to have the least amount of responsibilities and control over another adult.

> **HERE'S A QUICK** way to know if you need to create healthier boundaries: When asked about yourself, do you often respond by talking about others or have a hard time keeping the focus on yourself? Do you feel uncomfortable, anxious, nervous, or "not right" about doing things, but you find yourself doing them so someone else doesn't feel uncomfortable? Do you find yourself constantly holding back from asking for something you want? Do you find yourself over-apologizing? Do you find yourself always jumping in to fix things for others, even when they never asked for your help? If you said yes to any of these questions, they are signs that you need to create healthier boundaries.

I found that detachment was one of the best ways for me to create boundaries in my life. Honoring ourselves and those we love requires detachment. Detachment means separating ourselves emotionally from others. You wouldn't take it personally or blame someone you love who came down with a bad cold and canceled plans with you. You would simply be understanding. They were sick, so the plans changed. This is detachment. In the same way, we can set our personal boundaries with compassion. We can detach and allow the boundaries to do their job when someone upsets us or treats us poorly. Learning to detach often begins by learning to take a moment before we react. I call this the Power of the Pause.

When we pause,

we can ask ourselves questions like:

"Why do I want to say something right now?"

"How important is this?"

"Am I taking this personally?"

"Do I even need to respond to this?"

"Am I being clear and honest?"

Attachment, however, is the opposite. Attachment is not intimacy, nor is it a true connection. Attachment is control and it will suck the life out of you. When we don't detach, no matter what another says or does, we take it personally. We believe we are in control of everything, and when events go wrong, plans change, or other people behave differently than we would have hoped, we crumble or lash out. Before I had boundaries, this pattern of attachment would show up in two ways. I would either become a complete doormat, letting anyone and everyone walk all over me. Or I would become a relentless punisher, tearing through them like a tornado in the night. If you want to feel less attached to outcomes and more willing to detach, here are some of my favorite tips:

- *Don't give advice unless asked.* This is a hard one for me, especially in the work I do! A super simple way to hold myself accountable is that I wait for the question when someone may be telling me a story or sharing what's on their mind. If there isn't a question, I need not jump in with my thoughts.

- *Keep the focus on yourself.* When you keep the focus on you, you lose focus on the other person's behavior. You also decrease your desire to "jump in" and help, or worse, tell them what to do or how to act. This helps others experience their own choices and keeps you from trying to fix a person, place, or situation.

- *Get honest about why you want to speak.* A lot of times we will speak without being honest about why we feel the need to say something in the first place. Often, it comes from wanting to control or fix a feeling. It's important before you say something to ask yourself, *Why do I want to speak right now? What payoff am I wanting?* Is it because you want to be liked, right, admired, validated, or praised? Is it because you want to blame, control, or manipulate someone? Getting honest with yourself about why you want to speak is not meant to cause blame, shame, or judgment; it's meant to make you aware of your true intentions.

- *Leave the room/situation if you can't be quiet.* There have been many times when I have overstepped a boundary or gotten myself in a really bad situation because I couldn't zip my mouth! There is a time and place to speak your truth, and a time and place to listen. There's an acronym that I love called THINK, which stands for Thoughtful, Helpful, Inspiring, Necessary, and Kind. If what I want to say is not all of those things, then unless someone asked for my advice, it's better I stay quiet and listen.

- *Compliments before complaints.* It's natural for people to see the bad before they see the good. It is actually how our brain is wired. But when we start talking to ourselves and others with complaints instead of compliments, we stifle any chance of gratitude and appreciation emerging. If you can begin with a compliment over a complaint, it will help you detach in a loving way. Your relationships, communication, and entire life can change!

- *Let yourself off the hook.* Practice letting go of what you cannot change and give yourself some grace when needed,

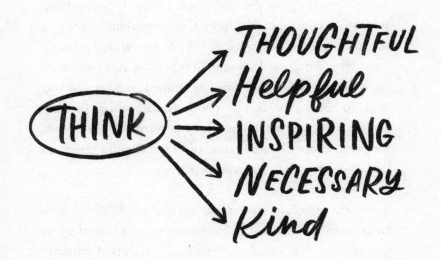

because most of the time, what you think is your problem is not your problem at all.

Although at first the answer might not be clear to us, over time it becomes easier to see. This distinction makes us better able to detach ourselves from the behaviors we find unacceptable while still showing compassion and love to ourselves, thus creating boundaries.

At first it may be hard to detach. We have often done so with resentment, silence, angry outbursts, and blame in the past. Mastering detachment with love takes time and practice. Even if we start badly, it's important to begin. But it is even more important to remember that establishing personal boundaries with another is not the same as building walls. We should focus on healing ourselves and our relationships with other people, not harshly distancing ourselves from those most precious to us. We must learn to allow people to be human, while knowing what to tolerate and not tolerate. When we detach with love, we accept others exactly as they are. And that is the most loving thing we can ever do.

AFFIRMATIONS TO SET BOUNDARIES

- I am worthy of love and can give it to myself.
- I choose to take care of myself and my needs first. It is not selfish.
- I own my actions. I am not responsible for yours or how you respond to mine.
- I can love without taking responsibility for your pain.
- I let go of the belief that I must take care of and save everyone in crisis. I am not that powerful.

HAVE NON-NEGOTIABLES

Creating non-negotiables is the foundation of self-care. You can't get what you want without self-care. Non-negotiables help us define our personal limits, while boundaries protect us. This involves determining for ourselves what we will and will not do or accept. It can be as simple as setting our bedtime at 10:00 p.m. or deciding not to tolerate abusive behavior. Non-negotiables help us know in advance what our options are and how we feel about them. When faced with a stressful situation where we may not be thinking clearly, we will have some idea of what's best for us. It is entirely up to us to determine what is acceptable and what is not. The same behavior that is intolerable to one person won't bother another person at all—which is why this work must be yours and yours alone.

Your non-negotiables do not dictate how other people should behave. Non-negotiables are not threats or forms of manipulation. They are simply facts that clearly define your boundaries. For example, a non-negotiable may sound like, "I will leave if I feel uncomfortable," rather than "I'd better not catch you doing something wrong," or "Promise me you won't do something wrong." There is always a right and perfect time to communicate your non-negotiables, but being honest about the intention is key. Whenever I know it is time to share a non-negotiable, I pause to be sure I'm prepared to follow through. There's so much power in pausing, while empty threats do nothing but diminish my credibility and self-esteem.

I have regretted sharing something too soon,

but I have never regretted pausing

before sharing something.

A non-negotiable doesn't mean you're trying to control or change someone, or that you're giving them an ultimatum. It means you are saying very clearly what you will and will not stand for.

ADVOCATE FOR YOURSELF

Self-advocacy means that you are able to tell people about your thoughts and feelings with full transparency. You are able to ask for what you need and want. You know your rights and you speak up for them. You no longer stay silent so that others can stay comfortable. Self-advocacy helps us examine, with honesty and courage, our personal understanding of security and our clarity of values.

I believe there is nothing nobler than knowing what our values are, putting them into practice, and having the realization that we are who we say we are.

We know this because we are in alignment with our integrity. Self-advocacy is the highest level of security. It's what brings us ultimate joy. This comes with understanding what security, values, and trust mean for you, so you can carry them out.

To me:

Security means creating a safe container to express my thoughts, feelings, and intentions.

Values are the measures I use to prioritize my needs and tell if I am getting out of life what I intend.

Trust means having a confident relationship with what is unknown.

YOUR TURN

Having Non-Negotiables

What are some of your non-negotiables in your business and personal relationships? What are your expectations and beliefs about how you want to be treated?

_____

_____

_____

Advocating for Yourself

Take some time to think about your values and how you define them. Then write them down in a journal or notebook. Here's a quick and extremely effective exercise I do with my clients on values.

What matters more to you than money and family? Make a list of everything that comes up for you.

_____

_____

_____

Now, ask yourself why, and write down the answers. Those answers are your values.

_____

_____

_____

With your values in mind, what are some steps you can take to advocate for yourself?

_____

_____

_____

CHAPTER FOUR

Find Your Purpose

The 6:00 a.m. phone call woke me up. "We're fired. He fired us," said Beth, the publicity business partner I had teamed up with after leaving corporate America.

"What?" I asked, rubbing my eyes, wondering, *Fired from what? By whom?* I was so confused.

"It's done," she said.

It was launch day for our client and he was in New York on a national press tour. There had been a double-booking issue that came up, which meant our client wasn't able to go live on a show. What I thought would be a happy phone call had just turned into the news that our client fired us.

Fired? I had never been fired in my life! How could he fire us? We'd gone above and beyond for him, working hard over nine months and sacrificing to make his book a priority. Getting him great press, doing all this work, killing ourselves for days on end. How did this happen?

As much as it stung to be fired, there was also a part of me that was relieved. The last year of doing book PR had been rough for me. I was burned out, tired, and felt like I was spinning my wheels only to be left empty and unfulfilled.

All of my time and energy being a solution provider for clients while trying to keep the passion alive had been coming to an end for quite some time. But I was afraid to believe it. *If I don't do this work, who am I? What will I do? How will I make money?* I could no longer hide from the truth.

When you can't do for yourself

what needs to be done, the world has

a funny way of doing it for you.

The passion that I once had for book publicity was fading fast. It no longer felt authentic. And by trying to force it through and not listen to myself, this was the result I was left with:

You're fired!

A few days later, I broke out in cystic hives from my head to my legs. They wouldn't go away. My dermatologist couldn't explain what was happening. My cortisol levels were shot, I couldn't sleep well, and I was clearly suffering from exhaustion. I didn't know what to do. I called my friend Alyshia and explained to her what happened, and she recommended that I speak to a life coach she knew.

A life coach?

I was hesitant. Not that I didn't believe in getting help, but I thought that was for people who were sick, or depressed, or going through a divorce. At the time, I was none of those things. The thought of seeking help through a coach had never occurred to me.

Not that I didn't know it existed, but I never thought I was someone who would ever benefit from a "coach." After all, I had a college degree, I had professional success working at an agency in corporate America, and now I was my own boss. I had gotten through my divorce and was happily remarried. What the heck could a coach do for me?

I took a call with the coach, Nicola, to hear about who she was and how she worked. She seemed great. And to my surprise, it felt right—though I couldn't place my finger on why.

As I got off the phone and looked in the mirror at my broken-out face and body, feeling the knot of depletion in my throat and the tears of exhaustion swelling my eyes, I thought, *Well, maybe a coach could do something for me.* I mean, my friend had seen a major shift working with one. And I knew other women who had as well. Perhaps if I could stay open-minded and not assume that I wasn't teachable, then maybe I could get out of my own way a little bit, learn a different perspective, and change some things.

Because at the end of the day, whatever I was doing wasn't working, no matter how much success I had, or how hard I worked, how many hours I put in, or how together my life appeared to be. Just because I wasn't living under a bridge or lying in a ditch with a needle in my arm didn't mean that I didn't need help.

You see, my origin story told me therapy was weird, asking for help was weak, and depression, addiction, and mental health challenges were a choice, not a disease or a byproduct of trauma.

So, of course, I was hesitant to show up and ask for help. I had been ashamed of it my whole life! I had the false belief that I had to know it all and that no one or nothing could help me as much as I could help myself.

That's the thing with denial; it runs deep. But there was one thing I could no longer deny: this coach had something I wanted. She had a thriving, purpose-driven career. She was helping women become better versions of themselves. She was authentic, charismatic, and magnetic. She made good money. Most of all, she had three things that I wanted most: joy, freedom, and peace.

Finally allowing myself to work with a coach helped me get clear on my true purpose, focus on the passions that fueled my purpose (and those that didn't), and gain the confidence I needed to create my very first online course, which became the foundation of the business I have today.

From there, I began working with more coaches and experts on the things in my life and business I wanted to strengthen. Soon I felt a positive shift in my friendships and my relationships. Working with a coach helped me create better boundaries, speak my truth confidently, and listen to others with more compassion.

Most important, it taught me a lifelong lesson:

If you want to change your life,

find support and help from people who

have the kind of life you aspire to have.

When I decided to be coached, I let my guard down. I could no longer be afraid to share my thoughts or ask tough and vulnerable questions around my peers. I needed to trust the process and be willing to receive it. I also learned that I didn't have it all figured out. You see, I always believed that I had really good ideas about how everyone in the world should think and feel, and if they would just listen to me, their world (and *the* world) would be a much better place. Well, shocking as it may have been, Julie Solomon did not have answers to all the world's problems.

I also learned that my purpose was creating a lasting impact in the lives of others so I can get what I want most: the freedom to live my life completely on my terms.

To be that example, I had to lead by example. That meant showing up in ways I never had before. It meant laying new foundations in my work and my relationships that would grant me greater stability. It meant investing in myself in ways I had never dreamed possible so I could achieve great clarity in my leadership power and how I influence others. It meant letting go of the old beliefs that were keeping me from living my life to its fullest.

Working with a coach, I also came to realize that my goal of constant achievement was destined to fail because it wasn't authentic. Nor was it realistic. It sets us up for failure, because when we hitch our purpose to an achievement-based outcome, our satisfaction is wholly dependent on whether we get that result. I did everything possible to help my client with his book launch, and due to circumstances beyond my control, he was still unhappy! I gave it everything I had and was totally passionate about his success. When he fired me, did I fail at my purpose in life? No! I simply hadn't predicted something that was outside of my control.

Your passion is the what.

Your purpose is the why.

That's when I came to realize there is a difference between passion and purpose: Your purpose is the difference and impact you want to make on the world. Your purpose comes from that steadfast voice within you that makes you want to change something about the community and world you live in. Your passion comes from your talents, personality, the timing in your life, education, experience, strengths, and interests. Simply put, your passion activates your purpose!

I chased the dream of a career in journalism and PR. I believed in the idea of "follow your passion" wholeheartedly. Fortunately, my passion for journalism and PR evolved into a thriving career. I went on to spearhead PR campaigns for dozens of bestselling authors and Grammy Award–winning artists. I traveled the world with clients, landing press for them that turned their dreams into reality. I achieved things I never thought were possible, all as a result of what I thought was *following my passion.*

However, from my own career experiences, I learned some profound lessons about "passion." First, I learned that passion is fleeting, ever evolving, and can be easily innovated. Purpose, on the other hand, will not only will give clarity and direction to your life, but it should long outlive you.

Passions and purposes are often conflated, but a passion is not the same as a purpose. For example, I have a passion for baking cakes and hiking in nature. I have a passion for the Tennessee Volunteers football team. But these passions don't fuel my greater purpose.

People get stuck when they think

every passion is their purpose.

There are passions that serve your purpose, but the two can also be mutually exclusive. You can have a driving purpose in life, and it doesn't have to be a passion; or you can have lots of passions that have nothing to do with your purpose.

That's why teenagers are standing in line to be on *American Idol.* They are passionate about singing. They think, *I'm going to be the next* American Idol. *It's clear this is my purpose in life because I'm passionate about it.*

But is it something you just like to do, or are even just really good at? Or is it contributing to your humanity?

There is a traditional school of thought where you need your passion to align with your purpose. But my view is a bit different.

Now if you have a hard time seeing this, just count how many crushes you had in school at one time or another. I doubt you're still crushing on little James from sixth grade—unless you ended up marrying him.

It's possible to be passionate about something one day, and then want to move and grow from it the next. If you had asked me a few years ago why I worked in PR, I would have said, "I love people. I love the action and fast-paced change of it all. I'm just so passionate about it!" But that wasn't why I did it. In fact, it took me years to figure out why.

I chose a career in PR to create impact and connect people. That was my purpose.

When I was able to make this distinction, it gave me clarity and a strategy to go after my new passion of creating my own business and services. I began looking for new opportunities. And that was when I discovered I had a knack for writing, teaching, and speaking, which evolved into a new set of passions. In ten years, those passions may look different, just as they did a decade ago. However, that doesn't change or affect my greater purpose of creating a lasting impact in the lives of others.

How many of us can, without a shadow of a doubt, say that we're going to be passionate about the same exact thing we are today a year from now, five years from now, ten years from now? We can't—it's impossible—because we can't predict the future, no more than we can predict our fleeting feelings and emotions. And what are passions if not strong emotions.

Your purpose stands alone. It doesn't come and go with the ebbs and flows of your emotions, career changes, or whatever you may be feeling today. Many of the women I coach show up with passion, but they don't know why it matters at a core, deep level. They don't know their purpose, or they've lost touch with it. Which is why they feel stuck and powerless.

Our purpose lays the foundation, our passions show us what's possible, and our actions make it all come to life.

Which is why figuring out your purpose is the foundation for everything you do.

Let's look at two ways to find your purpose, and two ways to figure out what your purpose should do.

I believe the goal is to build a business and a life

where you leave space for passions to pivot,

while always honoring your purpose.

IDENTIFY YOUR PURPOSE

So how do you find your purpose?

As we've covered, your purpose is your why. It's the foundation. It's the steadfast compass you need to keep yourself on track. You must give yourself the permission to bring it to life.

As simple as it may sound, it can be challenging. For some, it may take years or even an entire lifetime to find their purpose. Others may never bring it to life. This tends to happen when we try to live our purpose for other people. Often, people think their

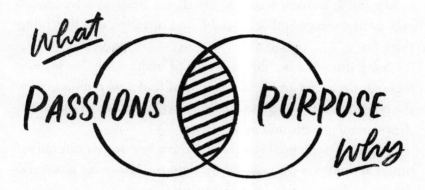

purpose must be for other people. That is not the case. Your purpose must be yours.

You know you have found your purpose when you get the feeling inside that excites you and warms your heart. Even though it may be a little scary, it makes you feel empowered and invigorated.

Even after I figured out my purpose, I still had to learn a very important lesson.

YOUR PURPOSE SHOULD BE STRONGER THAN YOUR EXCUSES

You aren't going to find your purpose unless you are ready to make it greater than your excuses and hold yourself accountable.

You are the captain of your own ship—no one else.

I've learned a lot from my early days of coaching. I can't even begin or get started if my clients don't work to figure out what their purpose is. Which is why it is always the first step we work on together. They must share their purpose with me. If they have it, great! If they don't or it's not strong or clear enough, then we work on that first.

My goal as a coach is to help my clients create massive impact and set up businesses that are stable and lucrative, and that bring them joy.

Doing this attracts a different type of leader. One that is more focused, clear, and ambitious. A type of leader who understands the type of results a purpose can bring, which leads to more confidence, more growth, and more money.

And that is why finding your purpose is key: so you can call on others around you who also have a purpose. Just as my coach did for me, and just as I do for so many others now.

That's what makes it great when you finally get what you want, because it was worth it. You earned it because the purpose was stronger. The reason for not giving up was stronger.

Suddenly everything becomes laser focused. When your purpose is stronger than your excuses, you don't waste as much time getting to work and making what you want happen.

YOUR PURPOSE SHOULD GIVE YOU CLEAR FOCUS

Something else that may get in your way when you're getting clear on your purpose is the addiction to distraction and hustle.

We have this false belief that constant work and productivity mean results, which in turn will give you purpose.

If you hear yourself saying, "I'm burned out. I don't know what to do," know that you're not alone.

This is a sign for you to slow down, just as I did when I was making my career shift and defining my real purpose.

I knew I had to make lasting changes when I was breaking out in hives. Living your purpose doesn't cause you to self-destruct. It builds you and holds you up during tough times.

I know many women who distract themselves with so much *doing*, so they don't have to do the transformational work, and then they're left with little to no changes or results.

If your purpose doesn't give you clear focus, you're doing it wrong. Although it can make you excited, it should also center you. Purpose is a steady anchor. It grounds and sustains you.

CRAFTING YOUR OWN PURPOSE

Suppose I asked you right now: What is your purpose? Would you be able to summarize it in a sentence or even one word? Do you know what it is? Is it strong enough to keep you from quitting? If you don't know what your purpose is, are you getting the coaching and support you need to figure it out?

I have watched people succeed and I can feel how powerful their purpose is. But I have also witnessed those who didn't quite make it, those with one foot in and one foot out, because their purpose wasn't compelling enough. I have helped them go a little bit deeper to get over their doubt and their frustration and really craft a purpose that is meaningful to them and will help them over the hump when things get tough.

And that's what I want to offer to you. But you may be wondering, *Julie, how do I figure out my purpose?*

The best way to figure out your purpose is to let curiosity be your superpower. You need not have perfect answers. There is no right or wrong. Your purpose can be in your family. It can be work related or personally driven. It can be wherever you're wanting to create the legacy in your life.

FINAL THOUGHTS ON FINDING YOUR PURPOSE

It's completely normal to want to resist figuring out your purpose. Getting clear on your purpose means shedding some nasty beliefs about your potential and capacity. It means showing up in a way you never have before. It's transformational, which can feel scary.

I know what it's like to feel confused, helpless, lost, and frustrated. I know what it's like to feel shackled by victimhood. So when I feel doubt and frustration, and I'm upset, I think about that one person I haven't helped yet. I think about that one person who feels hopeless. I think about the woman who's in a job she hates. I think about the woman who keeps focusing on the silly projects and not getting anywhere. I think about the woman who's suffering at her own expense unnecessarily. I think about the woman who is in a situation where she has to ask permission from someone else to invest in herself, and she doesn't want to live that way anymore.

To me, the opposite of powerlessness is freedom. That is what drives me: to help people achieve the freedom they want in life. And that can look very different for each of us. For some people, it's retiring with their husbands or their wives. For others, it is being able to move into a bigger house, pay for their kids to go to college, or help their parents out.

But when you feel the conviction of your purpose—so much that you feel it in your bones—you know that you're onto something. You know you're living your purpose because nothing will stop you. You believe all the sacrifices you're making and all the pain you endure are worth it.

When you know your purpose, you'll want to be more connected with the real, authentic you. All the doubt and frustration in the world won't even be able to sway you from it.

Make sure you have the deepest, most important purpose you can possibly have, so you can have a tool to get you through the hard times. Because I must tell you: on the other side is a life you can only imagine at this point.

Once you have your purpose, you need the clarity and confidence to execute it. And that's where we are headed next.

YOUR TURN

Below are a series of deep-dive questions I ask each of my clients to help them get clear on their purpose.

Purpose

Why do you get up every day and do your work?

_____

_____

_____

What about you makes people feel great about themselves?

_____

_____

_____

Why is your ultimate dream important to you?

_____

_____

_____

What kind of impact do you want to make?

_____

_____

_____

Using your notes from these four questions, write as many compelling reasons as you can for why you show up every day.

_____

_____

_____

Now, omit all but three reasons. Only leave the most important three.

_____

_____

_____

Now, omit all but one. The one that is left is your purpose. What is your purpose?

_____

_____

_____

An easy way to being sure you have landed on the right purpose is to complete this sentence:

My purpose, _____,
is alive when I feel _____.

Here are some examples from myself and my clients:

My purpose, impact, is alive when I feel freedom.

My purpose, connection, is alive when I feel recognized.

My purpose, independence, is alive when I feel secure.

My purpose, fulfillment, is alive when I feel joy.

My purpose, empowering others, is alive when I feel gratitude.

Do you need to reword your purpose?

_____

_____

_____

What excuses do you think could get in your way of following your purpose?

_____

_____

_____

How do you plan to overcome these excuses?

_____

_____

_____

Passions

What are your main passions? Think about what lights you up, brings you joy, and makes you feel excited, expansive, and maybe even nervous to do. Pick one to three.

_____

_____

_____

What is the ONE BIG PASSION you've wanted to start or do for a while now that you just can't stop thinking about? (*Just pick one for now.*)

_____

_____

_____

What do you have experience in already that could support your ONE BIG PASSION?

_____

_____

_____

PART TWO

Taking Action

CHAPTER FIVE

Becoming the Visionary

I t was 2015. I was sitting in my makeshift home office trying to read a blog post, check emails, and help my son put together a puzzle he got at the zoo when one of my favorite online marketers at the time, Melyssa, announced in an income report blog post that she had made one million dollars in less than twelve months.

A year, people.

I didn't even know that was possible. My jaw dropped. I said it out loud: "One. Million. Dollars." I felt something shift inside. Melyssa mentioned it not as if she'd won the lottery or found the cure for cancer, but as though it were normal and doable. I got the sense that she would do it again. The next year she launched a wildly successful course, scaled services, and built out affiliate marketing opportunities. She more than doubled her revenue from the previous year. There was nothing impossible about anything she was doing. I guess I knew it was possible to make millions of dollars in one year, but the problem was it had never even occurred to me to do it myself. I'd always fantasized what it would be like to have a million dollars, but the "how" was never in the story line of those fantasies.

It was like a language I didn't understand or a culture I'd never been exposed to. As soon as I knew it was possible, it became my new goal. I began to see everything differently. My actions changed. I told myself, "It's not what I need to *have* before I can start, or what work I need to *do*, but who I need to *be* first! I need to be the person who works on making a million dollars in a year. What do they focus on? What are their daily goals? What access do they create for themselves and what network of people do they make sure to know? That's who I need to become!"

And that's when I realized something that changed my entire life.

Successful people work on *becoming*

the person they need to be in the future,

so they get the results they want *today*.

You read that correctly. I didn't say that I needed results first, so I could get what I wanted in the future. That kind of thinking lacks imagination, vision, and faith.

Let's put this into action: Imagine the woman you want to be. Think of what her daily life looks like. Notice what her habits, behavior, and routines would be. Write them down. Next, start showing up to those habits and routines. Start building them, step by step, one day at a time. You don't wave a magic wand and become her. You don't wait for some person, place, or thing to give her to you. You build her.

So start building.

Two years after I read Melyssa's first million-dollar income report, I made $1 million in my business. Since that day, I have not stopped talking about impact, influence, and freedom. I'm so thankful Melyssa shared her income out loud to teach me what was possible.

I saw something in a way that I never had before. It gave me a vision.

CLEAR MIND EQUALS CLEAR VISION

Think of this vision as a portal. It is how everything starts channeling through you and coming together. You make it happen by being keenly aware of your thoughts. Your vision takes your purpose and puts it into action.

You see, it wasn't until I took the imaginative leap and put myself in that situation where I could do it that the dots were connected. And that imaginative leap was possible because I gave myself the permission to think in a new way.

This is where the real, transformational work happens. When your mind is clear, new ideas start flowing. It feels magical.

That said, you'll need to use these ideas to build a plan. We'll talk about this in more detail in chapter 6, but you wouldn't attempt to build the house of your dreams without a blueprint. Before you even reach for a hammer, you need to have deep conversations about your vision for the house. The same thing goes for your business and your life.

More important, you need to build a plan that makes sense *for you*. Before I learned this, I had always believed that if I just imitated what someone else was doing, I could also achieve their success. This would always leave me more confused and burned out. I would always wonder: *Why can't I make this happen? I'm trying so hard and doing everything that person is doing!*

But it wasn't what Melyssa was doing that was the key. It wasn't the business model or services she was providing. It was the way she thought.

I had been doing it wrong for so long, and that's when it clicked.

I didn't need to imitate what she did.

I needed to imitate how she thought.

I want you to be honest right now: What are your thoughts about your business? Are they thoughts that are supporting your vision and your goals? Are they thoughts that are keeping you stuck? When clients come to work with me inside my mastermind SHINE, typically their thoughts are, *I can't handle this. It's too overwhelming. I'm exhausted. This isn't fun anymore.*

One of the things that I often say to my clients is, "The results you are seeing from your business are just the thoughts you have about your business coming to life."

So if you're not thinking about your business or your life in a positive, wonderful, awesome way, there's no way you can create that result you want. I recommend writing down all the thoughts you're currently having about your business, company, team, project, your spouse, because they are important. (I'll touch on an exercise later in this chapter to help you do just that!) Just as we explored in chapter 1 how important it is to bring awareness to the things that are holding you back, to accept them, and move to action, you can use those same 3A's to examine your own thoughts and how they are currently affecting your life and work. This isn't just a soft skill that I'm trying to teach you. It's a deliberate, proactive step you must master.

Your thoughts will also create a lot of feelings. We often think that business is stressful, growing a business is overwhelming, working with people is frustrating. That is never the case. You are responsible for all your own emotions; you're responsible for causing them. You cause everything you feel. You cause your own reality. No one person or thing can make you feel anything, which means you can change your state and your environment. This is such a huge, beautiful shift of awareness and understanding. You have the choice to feel whatever you want whenever you want.

For example, when we first start working together, many of my clients feel overwhelmed. When you start to create more growth and impact in the world, the natural thought process is, *This is too much; I can't handle it.*

Overwhelm is just a feeling we are choosing when we are resisting the reality of where we are today.

Things are happening and moving in the right direction; your thoughts and feelings are just lagging.

I want you to have a more effective state of mind, which will create an effective environment to achieve what you want. Here are some of the emotions that we need to be generating for ourselves in order to be effective:

Confidence: You gain confidence by testing out new things and gradually getting stronger and more skilled at them. You also feel much more confident if you are aligned with your purpose (chapter 4). When you have a clear purpose, you can move mountains.

Patience: You gain more patience by accepting what is today, not trying to make it be something it isn't, and admitting you don't know what is best. In chapter 1, we used the 3A's to figure out what we had control over and what we didn't. Using our abilities to bring awareness to our thoughts and emotions, we realized what we could accept and then take the desired action.

Resilience: When we're resilient we can bounce back quickly. We can pivot, change when required, and conserve our energy (rather than use it to fight battles that can't be won). One of the things we all learned during the pandemic of 2020 was resilience. So much was out of our control. Once we got to the place of awareness that this is how the world is now, and we alone weren't going to change it, we could take the desired action. Waiting around for it to "return to normal" wasn't an option most of us had. We all had to adjust. Many of us pivoted overnight—working from home, homeschooling, and even changing the way we ran our households or did business. Some of us realized we were thriving. Some of us realized we were struggling. But most of us realized we had no choice but to adjust, because if we were fixated on one outcome, we would be sorely disappointed. And one of the feelings that helped us do so was:

Resoluteness: You gain resoluteness by deciding and sticking with it, even if you can't control or predict the outcome. It's not about being right; it's about taking action. Most of us had no idea what we were doing at the beginning of the pandemic. Every day required something new, but we were all connected by the same emotion: we were determined and resolved to survive it—not just the virus, but all the uncertainty. And what helped most of us stay resolute was:

Focus: We were all able to zero in on what really mattered—our health, our families, our kids' educations, our desires to live our lives in "the new normal," especially if we were sick of the "normal" to begin with.

A vision without focus is just a fantasy.

Having focus helps you get clear on what you want. It helps you define obstacles. With focus, priorities fall into place automatically. Suddenly, it's easy to see what is stopping you or standing in your way when you have focus. It gives you the courage to drop the dead weight that no longer serves you.

HOW IMPORTANT IS IT?

I have noticed that the more I work with clients who are creating impact and scaling successful careers, the more ease and focus they have, the more success they have and money they make. Because none of this is the end of the world. When we get so worked up over the littlest things, we're completely ineffective and we burn ourselves out.

That is why the question "How important is it?"
is such a vital one in my life and in my success.

You must remember the energy you are using to get what you want must be positive energy. If you are fueling yourself with negative energy and thinking every little detail is worth stressing over, you're always going to end up with a negative, self-perpetuating result. That is why we must bring our thoughts back to our greater vision. There's a great quote by President Barack Obama that says, "[If] you're worrying about yourself—if you're thinking: 'Am I succeeding? Am I in the right position? Am I being appreciated?'— then you're going to end up feeling frustrated and stuck. But if you can keep it about the work, you'll always have a path. There's always something to be done."

DEALING WITH RESISTANCE

Something important we must realize when creating our vision: our origin story and limiting beliefs don't like it. This is when we go into what I called earlier the "resistance spin." When our limiting beliefs meet our vision, they kind of freak out. So we begin making lists of reasons and excuses why we can't achieve something or move up to the next level. We literally resist momentum. As psychologist Carl Jung said, "What you resist persists."

Fearful people who can't think critically hear something and freak out. We don't want to be those people. We want to be the people who can reason things out. We want to be the people who overcome the resistance spin. We want to be critical thinkers.

But, if you already closed the door, why are you going to reopen it for someone from the past—or for past ideas, perspectives, and energies that are back to tease, test, or trick you? No. You don't need it. You've already leveled up your clarity and confidence. You've already learned and grown from that limiting belief. But our minds love to be loyal to our origin story. So there will be times during this transformation when you're going to be like, "Uh, what do I do when the fear creeps in?" You must think critically and openly.

WHEN THE ORIGIN STORY CREEPS BACK IN

Recently I was talking to my client Valerie about this fear around living out our purpose. She rattled off a number of her fears: "Julie, my business has always been like a part-time thing for me. And my husband is by far the moneymaker for our family. We don't rely on money that I make to live; I still want to contribute to our family. And I have a need inside of me that I want to contribute to my community and the world. It feels good for me to do that too. But I feel like I'm trying to find the balance now between me wanting to go all in on this almost more for selfish reasons, such as to give back to the community and do something that makes me feel good. Also, I want to contribute financially to my family or at least feel like I am. But like it's all the competing, you know, priorities of like the kids and my family's needs? And so I'm just kind of managing, you know, a lot of making sure I have enough left of me to give to them as well. But I also feel like I need to make sure I am financially independent in case anything ever happens, and my husband isn't capable of working."

I told her I thought it was interesting that she used the word *selfish* to describe her desire to contribute. I asked her if she thought her husband felt selfish when he worked and contributed to the family. She said, "No, I think he feels like it's an obligation."

That's when I shared with Valerie this idea of how a lot of us view financial hierarchy in our marriages and families and how our origin stories can create fear in our lives. If your spouse makes more than you, then it would feel only natural to prioritize his work over anything else. But does this mean that we don't live out our own vision and dreams? Do we keep our businesses small so other businesses can thrive? And what about the kids and their needs? Do we cut back the hours so we can give more time to them, since our husbands' jobs are more important than ours? Where do we draw the line of compromise?

I think this feeling is a symptom of how each one of us, in our own unique way, was raised. The financial hierarchy piece can keep people from getting what they want because they don't want to lose money, or they don't want to feel like they're losing family time. And I think that it all comes from this idea of what was mirrored and modeled to us when we were being raised and is what we know to be true. You live what you know.

Why does becoming the financial breadwinner for the family feel like a choice for a woman and an obligation for a man?

If we were raised to believe that, typically, it is the man's obligation to provide for the family (which means his work is more important than ours), then of course we are always going to be playing second fiddle and never self-actualizing our own vision for success.

Of course, we're going to stay super small because that's what the world has told us to do. We're going to be afraid to shine bright. We're going to believe that our spouses/partners/fill-in-the-blanks are more than capable of actualizing their vision over ours. Which then leaves room for the guilt of taking away time from other important people and things—like children. The martyrdom of motherhood is back to rear its ugly head!

I'm not contributing financially. My work doesn't matter in the grand scheme of things. Those words are powerful. It's like an energetic spell.

You are never going to commit to a vision if that's your belief.

The truth is that the sky's the limit. There is no ceiling for what you're capable of, except for the one you create for yourself.

I asked Valerie if she had this conversation with her husband or ever told him about her vision to contribute and help support her family, and to want the joy and pride that comes from that and working toward creating a plan around that. She said she hadn't but that she was open to the idea and wanted to think through what that could look like.

These challenges give us an opportunity to re-parent ourselves and re-parent how we approach our vision for success. How do we let ourselves off the hook? We could ask ourselves the following questions:

- What can you change if you can't change this?
- How many hours a day do you need and want to invest in your family or other commitments to take care of priorities *and* feel good?
- How much money do you need to make to feel like you are contributing to your greater vision?

THOUGHT DOWNLOAD

The way I do this is with a thought download. Many people teach variations of a thought download, but from my understanding of it, it originated with Brooke Castillo, founder of The Life Coach School. Basically, a thought download is a journaling practice where you write down all the thoughts you have about your situation, whether business related or personal. You don't hold back or edit yourself. Just write whatever thoughts you think are true about your situation and see what it reveals to you.

I believe that the thought download is the first step, because that's what gives you the awareness. From there you can accept what you can and cannot change. And then you can create the vision that works for you. This is all about self-actualization. It helps you get comfortable with the unknown.

FIND A PATH TO VISION

The beauty of a vision is that it can be applied to virtually every aspect of your life, not just your work. It brings about the clarity we all need to succeed, and it makes decisions easier and more effective. It helps you know what your priorities are. It helps cut your workload in half by working smarter, not harder. It gives you time back with your family and friends. But it requires that you, as the leader, be extremely clear about why you're working in the first place.

A simple way to find a path to vision is by answering one question: What is the goal?

That question should be applied to anything you do, whether it's your business, a meeting, a new hire, or a project. For me, my vision is more of my long-term focus, whereas my goals are for short-term focus. Here are some examples:

- What is the goal of this meeting?
- What is the goal of this project?
- What is the goal of creating this new service?
- What is the goal of this phone call or email?

Understanding the goal keeps the vision clear. It reminds me of going to the optometrist to get your annual eye exam. The goal is to be able to read the letters on the screen. If you can't, that means your vision isn't clear and that you need help to see better. The same applies here. If you can't see the goal, your vision isn't clear.

It's amazing what becomes clear when we just take a little bit of time to answer the goal question. Yet this simple exercise is often overlooked. When most people are growing their business, they get so consumed with reacting to daily challenges, such as how much money they are or aren't making, that they forget to stay focused.

These reactive, challenging moments happen to us all. They will come whether you want them to or not, so it's best to be prepared.

I want you to take some time to answer that question and write down your vision. To help you get you started, I'll share my vision: it is to support leaders who are ready to accelerate their impact and create iconic success.

The goal of every piece of work I create, meeting I take, podcast I record, person I hire, stage I speak on, and book I write is to directly support that vision. I will ask myself: *Does this support my vision? Does it help leaders create more impact? Does it grow a network that creates the growth I'm looking for? Is it going to get me closer to creating iconic success and building a true legacy?* If it doesn't, then I don't do it. It's that simple.

One of the important things you want to remember when you're writing your vision is that it needs to be about what *you* will do and create, and not what you hope someone else will gain from it.

For example, I hope to help my clients build strong relationships and make money. But that's not my vision. My vision is about the support, which is my part to play in their results. But it's not the result. Their result is part of their own vision.

So, when you sit down to write this, make sure your vision doesn't depend on what someone else is doing or the amount of success they may, or may not, achieve.

Also, your vision may not happen overnight, or this year, or in the next five years. And that is okay if you're keeping true to your vision and working toward it each day, realistically.

You get to pick what that vision is and then attach it to the metrics of the revenue, profit, or growth that will support that vision.

What is your goal? Simply write it down on a piece of paper. You may need to brainstorm in order to narrow it down to just one sentence. It doesn't have to be perfect. And once you have it, you need to ask yourself every day: *Am I fulfilling my vision?*

YOUR TURN

Thought Download

In the space provided, write down all the thoughts you have about your situation. Don't hold back. Don't edit. Don't judge what you're writing. Whatever you think, write it down.

_____

_____

_____

Now that you have all the thoughts written, make a list of the top five feelings you have about these thoughts.

_____

_____

_____

Make a list of the top five feelings you would _like_ to feel.

_____

_____

_____

When you feel the way you want to feel, what kind of thoughts do you think you will have?

_____

_____

_____

Creating Your Vision

Creating a vision is a vital step in successfully getting what you want.

Answering the following questions will help you create your one-sentence vision for your business or your life. You can use it for both.

For example, here is my one-sentence vision statement for my business:

My vision is to support leaders who are ready to accelerate their impact and create iconic success.

And here is the one-sentence vision statement for my life:

My vision is to trust in a power greater than myself and be a prisoner of nothing.

To begin, here are some questions to help you brainstorm:

What is your goal?

_____

_____

_____

What is the contribution you want to make?

_____

_____

_____

What aspirations do you have for your work? Your life?

_____

_____

_____

What do you hope someone says about the work you do?

_____

_____

_____

After spending time reflecting on your answers, write your one-sentence vision here:

_____

_____

_____

Post your vision somewhere you can see it daily. I have mine posted on my computer screen, so I see it every day. It's best to have it memorized so you can easily share it.

CHAPTER SIX

Creating a Blueprint for Success

D o you ever feel like you are on the cusp of something great, but there just seems to be something that keeps getting in the way? This is how I felt for about a decade. As I mentioned earlier, when I graduated from college in 2007, I moved straight to New York City. I had no job. I had no friends. I was propelled to go there by this small voice within me saying that I wanted to experience more. I wanted to see more. I tried for months to get a job and was just doing whatever I could on the side to make ends meet. And finally, three months in, after surfing on a friend of a friend of a friend's couch, I got a job as an assistant to a music publicist at one of the top music PR agencies in the country. I was paid $25,000 a year in New York City with $30,000 of student loan debt. I worked nonstop, but I loved that job! I loved doing something new that was truly mine. I got to travel and experience incredible life-changing opportunities. But eventually, it just wasn't financially feasible for me to do it anymore.

So I moved back to Nashville in 2008, went to work for a publishing house doing book publicity, and got to work with some incredible authors. But a few years in, I began to feel a tug that this wasn't "it." I couldn't quite place my finger on why, but it felt like it was holding me back instead of moving me forward. I was terrified. I still had my debt at the time and was also going through a divorce and found myself in a scary place of *what am I meant to be doing?*

I couldn't understand why I wasn't satisfied but knew that I could no longer turn down the volume on what I truly wished for and desired, because I so desperately wanted to please everyone else around me. Once I could no longer ignore this voice inside me, I went out on my own as a publicist, using the connections I had made over the previous years to find work.

I tried to focus on what I had gotten paid for in my previous jobs—things I had proven that I could do and get paid to do. At the same time, I started to take inventory, asking myself:

What do I want?

What is keeping me from getting that?

They seem to be simple questions, but I would always avoid them because they were painful to answer. Answering them forced me to peel back a lot of layers and confront how I was keeping myself miserable and continuing to believe untrue things about myself.

During this time in 2012, I met my now-husband, moved to LA, and we very quickly got pregnant. Leaving everyone I knew for a place where I had no friends brought me back to my time in New York when I had to figure out how to survive, grow, and make friends.

I started wondering how I could surround myself with people who inspired me—people I could learn from and be of service to.

At the time, people were beginning to make a living as bloggers and influencer marketers. So, to feel connected to this new city and find a creative outlet, encouraged by my friend Angela, I started blogging on top of the PR work I was doing. Blogging taught me a lot about creativity and writing.

Thanks to my years of publicity work, I quickly began to monetize my blog. Before long, women I met in the new blogging community were asking me how I was doing it. They wanted to have success with their blogs as well!

All I was doing was applying what I knew from my years of working in PR and marketing. Soon, I learned what these women really needed from me, which was help in pitching themselves so they could make more money and get their names and brands out to the world. I began to change my content to focus on that need.

And here's the thing: I didn't have a big audience. I didn't have a lot of people reading my blog or following me on social media. I had no type of email marketing strategy or paid advertising.

I was simply listening to whatever community there was around me. What were they saying when I would go out and have coffee, or go to meetups or networking opportunities? I would look at someone and think, *Hmm. Maybe this is the type of person that I need to be serving. Am I capable of serving them with the expertise I currently have?*

Though I didn't have an audience, one still existed. Somebody else may have already built it or maybe it was a friend of a friend whom I could invite to lunch. I would ask them what their challenges were when it came to growing and monetizing their brand, and then boom. I would get all these ideas that I could turn into content.

I started doing one-off blog posts about overcoming the challenges that people were having. I provided easy step-by-step solutions to these challenges. I started getting more curious when people asked, "How can you help me more? How can I get more of this? Your blog posts are great, but what's the next step?"

So, I asked myself: *How can I solve their problem?*

The answer was Pitch It Perfect, my first online course, which debuted in 2016 and is still going strong today. Pitch It Perfect helps people learn how to pitch themselves and negotiate for higher pay, whether that's for new collaborations, partnerships, or monetizing their social media platforms. The program also helps people land more clients and get media for themselves. It lays out exactly how to pitch yourself to get whatever it is you want and get paid for it.

When I created Pitch It Perfect, I didn't know how to create a course. I didn't know how to do workshops and record webinars. I didn't know how to run Facebook ads. I sure as heck didn't have extra money falling from the sky to do any of this.

It took years of fine-tuning and tweaking. When I would make a little bit of money, I'd invest a little bit more back in it. I launched Pitch It Perfect with pretty much nothing other than my knowledge, tested formula, and a laptop.

And now, years later, that program has gone on to generate millions of dollars in revenue. Most important, it has impacted thousands of lives. It's allowed students to go full-time with their dream careers. More students than I can name have quit their nine-to-five jobs to make six figures a year doing what they loved the most. It has gotten my students on the covers of magazines and billboards in Times Square. It's given people the chance to build their dream home and buy their parents brand-new cars. This program that came from nothing more than curiosity and action has helped people generate more than $8 million in revenue to date and countless opportunities for impact and growth for their lives, families, and businesses. That kind of impact is something I could have never imagined.

MY BLUEPRINT FOR this success was created with these steps.

- Step 1: I started where I was, with what I had.
- Step 2: I listened for what a specific group of people said they needed and didn't try to solve every problem for everyone.
- Step 3: I made sure I could be the solution provider of those needs.
- Step 4: I allowed myself to pivot my direction and created services and offers around those needs.
- Step 5: I was consistent. I continued to level up and tweak the blueprint for years to come based on the needs of a specific group of people.

This is my blueprint for success, and I want to walk you through how to create your own. Now I want to note that some of you reading this don't need help growing your businesses, but I want to encourage you to take this blueprint in, even if you're not an entrepreneur, because so many of the concepts can be applied to any goal that you're trying to achieve, especially if you want to grow your influence and impact.

If this is something that speaks to you then this blueprint will help you achieve your goals—no matter what they are.

You already have a clear vision that we established in chapter 5. If you don't, go back and do the work. You can't create a blueprint without a vision. When a person goes to see an architect to build a house, the architect doesn't hand over a blueprint. A good one asks you what you want your house to look like, what style, what feel, what kind of structure. Architects can't possibly give you a blueprint for what you want if you don't tell them your vision. There is simply no skipping this step. Remember: It doesn't have to be about having a million dollars. It could be living with a beautiful view with zero debt and going after what makes you happy and secure.

I believe growing a business and making as much money as I want allows me to make positive contributions to the world.

HOW TO BUILD YOUR OWN BLUEPRINT

I want you to start thinking about your own business as it stands right now. Where are you in terms of growth, and what else do you need to grow?

The following five steps are the exact framework I used to build my business. You'll have a chance to work the steps in the "Your Turn" worksheet.

Step 1: Offer

Starting where you are today, with what you currently have, consider the following questions.

- What is your expertise?
- What do people typically come to you for?
- What are you great at that someone else would find extremely valuable?

The answers you give will be the basis for your offer. In order to figure out what kind of offer to create, you need to think of it as if you're selling someone their dream come true. If you can offer someone their dream, everyone wins.

Step 2: Prospects

Think about that one person for whom you are providing a solution. Notice I said *one* person: you cannot solve every problem for everyone, nor should you try.

Now that you've focused on one person, ask yourself: What are their challenges, beliefs, and goals? What is their dream come true? What do they want more than anything that you can provide?

Here are some examples of what my clients shared about their prospects:

My prospect wants to lose weight by cutting out sugar and alcohol from their diet.

My prospect wants interior design done for them at an affordable rate.

My prospect wants super delicious vegan and gluten-free cupcakes.

My prospect wants a better relationship with their spouse.

My prospect wants to feel more organized and less cluttered in their home.

Step 3: Results

It's not enough to promise a dream come true to your prospects. You need to be able to realistically provide what they need and deliver tangible results.

What are the best ways you can do that? What are the results you (or your services) promise? For example: Is it a service, program, method, or product that you can create to give your prospects what they need?

Step 4: Permission to Pivot

Note that the needs of your prospects can change over time. Give yourself permission to pivot as needed. Also, in order to be able to meet your clients' needs when they change, you'll need to figure out what may be holding you back from pivoting. You may also need to give up a project (or something else) in order to make that pivot successfully.

Step 5: Consistency

The way we reach a goal is by making consistent choices every day, over time. This includes leveling up for your prospects, tweaking your blueprint over the years as you continue to meet your prospects' needs.

YOUR BLUEPRINT CHALLENGES

Now, sometimes my clients tell me they want to avoid working on one of these. Which one do you think it is?

It's the *prospects*. See, in order to have prospects, which is a potential customer, you are going to have prospects that become customers, and prospects that don't. Which means, you are going to have people say no to you. And that's where I see so many of my clients get stuck.

CHALLENGE #1: Learn from the noes. This is one of the secrets that many people don't know. They hear "no" and just shut down instead of getting curious and using it as a growth opportunity. They don't like it; they take it personally. So, what do they do? They avoid getting noes, which means they avoid getting prospects, which means they make less impact. You have to ask yourself, *Why would someone say no to me?* You must figure out what it is. Are you making the wrong offer? Are you offering it to the wrong prospect? Whether or not they buy from you is not as important as how much you are learning from every prospect you talk to. Now if you're not making offers and you're not getting any feedback, you're not learning anything. You're just hiding in the corner. Once you recognize that noes move you forward, you start learning how to overcome your prospects' limiting beliefs about themselves. Then, you learn to use that to make better offers.

CHALLENGE #2: You must be offering something to somebody who wants it and will happily pay you for it. There are people out there who want what you can offer. Most don't want to pay you for it. However, some will. Your job is to find those who will. Have you ever walked the streets of New York City when it started raining buckets and suddenly, out of nowhere, there are vendors on every corner selling umbrellas? They know people are going to be drenched and that they will be willing to pay because they can't get an umbrella anywhere else, and they need it right now. They are soaked, annoyed, and still have a long walk. If you've ever paid ten dollars for a flimsy umbrella in a rainstorm, you understand the results that can come from meeting people where they are and offering them what they want. When you make the right offer to the right prospect, there's no limit to how big you can become.

CHALLENGE #3: You have to QTIP your feedback. QTIP stands for "Quit Taking It Personally." You can't take it personally when someone tells you no, or doesn't think your services are good, or gives whatever feedback they have for you. As soon as you take it personally, you're going to become exhausted, and you'll miss your opportunity to learn something important. No experience is wasted. There's no limit to how much money you can make. I've had clients make six figures in less than ninety days because they had the right offer, they pitched it to the right prospect, they focused on the results, learned from their noes, and were consistent to the point that their blueprint became repeatable.

DEALING WITH IMPOSTOR SYNDROME

One of the things I notice with entrepreneurs who start to gain some success is a lot of self-sabotage, what people refer to as the impostor syndrome. *Oh my gosh, what is happening? Why am I so successful? I shouldn't be here. I don't have enough talent and experience. Everyone is going to find out I am just a fraud.* And they start freaking out and sabotaging themselves.

I think with every single client I have coached, we touch on this at some point. They think, *Okay, Julie, when are the real experts coming to call me out?*

I have a client who made $3 million last year from her blog. She was able to buy her dad a car and set up college funds for her children. On our coaching call, she looked right at me and said, "Julie, people are going to figure out I don't know what the hell I'm doing."

One of the things you want to do about impostor syndrome is admit it to yourself. It's normal to feel this way, but I also want you to know that you need to continuously admit that's how you're feeling to yourself, so that you can move through it. It's part of the process, and it's never going to go away. If you keep setting bigger and bigger goals for yourself, you'll always be stepping into the next version of yourself, and it will be a full-on identity crisis, which will make you feel like an impostor. So, plan on it.

BE YOUR OWN PUBLICIST

An important piece when creating your blueprint for success is that it's your responsibility to be your own #1 fan, your own publicist, your own cheerleader.

Because here is the truth: it is no one else's job to make sure you are seen and heard and to make sure your work and message is put in front of everyone who needs it. I can't even begin to tell you how many times I have worked with clients, authors, influencers, and experts who are shocked by this truth. They always think some magical marketing fairy is going to fly down from the sky and make all their PR dreams comes true. As a publicist I am here to tell you, it doesn't work that way.

I don't care how many publicists you think you can hire or how much money you think you can throw at advertising and marketing to get that job done. Yes, those things can help, but they aren't the one-size-fits-all to your success.

At the end of the day, that job is yours, and yours alone.

Don't be afraid to shine bright and scream your expertise from the rooftops. In many ways, it's easier not to. It's easier to hide. It's easier not to be extraordinary, not to stand out, to be ignored. Yes, there'll be fewer opinions of you. There will also be less money for you and less impact you're making in the world.

A lot of people look at me and see someone with influence. They come to me and want me to speak on their stages and partner with them. They want to be on my podcast because they see an opportunity for greater exposure. But in their mind, the reason I'm an influencer is not because I have followers, or because I was a publicist, or because I know influential people. It's because I have the courage to be who I am to stand out from the crowd.

That courage is what gives you leadership. It's what gives you power. I'm willing to put myself out there and experience both sides of the struggle and the success. I want to get to the next level of impact and freedom—I believe that helps other people do the same. And I think it's really fun! Why not? Why not see what we can do with these lives of ours? Life is fleeting, so let's enjoy the ride.

You want to be successful? Then be uncomfortable. Be vulnerable. Hear the word "no" more without taking it personally. Ask for what you need and for what you want. Be willing to stand out and think bigger. Be willing to let go of people, places, things, and ideas that no longer serve you.

Be willing to SHINE.

MAKE YOUR PIVOT PRACTICAL

I've heard from so many people who say that they've been inspired by my work and want to reevaluate their nine-to-five jobs over the last couple of years. They feel stuck somewhere they no longer wish to be in their careers. Of course, money is the number one thing that keeps them from making the leap. I would be a total liar if I didn't say that this was my number one concern too. My parents come from humble beginnings and have lived parts of their lives with little money. That reality was hardwired into me, so I didn't just throw caution to the wind and start from scratch. I had a full-time job that allowed me the flexibility to work on a side hustle and pivot that to a full-time business once I was ready. When I hear people blithely telling everyone to follow their dreams, I feel like it's important to say the rest of that sentence. Follow your dreams, and make sure you also give them a realistic chance to survive. I'm not here to tell you what you may want to hear. That, if you stay true to your dreams, they will remain true to you. I will say this, though—the one thing I've learned is that it's never too late to pivot toward a new possibility that gets you one step closer to what you want. This blueprint is the first step.

YOUR TURN:
CREATING YOUR OWN BLUEPRINT

Offer

What is your expertise? What do people typically come to you for? What are you the absolute best at that someone else would find extremely valuable?

_____

_____

_____

Prospects

What do your prospects want? What are your prospects' challenges, beliefs, and goals? What is their dream come true? What do they want more than anything that you can provide?

_____

_____

_____

Results

Can you realistically provide what they need? If yes, what are the best ways you can do that? What are the results you (or your services) promise? For example: Is it a service, program, method, or product that you can create to give your prospects what they need?

_____

_____

_____

Permission to Pivot

What work or project do you need to let go of or remove today that is holding you back for serving the prospects?

_____

_____

_____

Consistency

What needs to happen consistently for you to reach your goals?

_____

_____

_____

CHAPTER SEVEN

Pitch It Perfect

I decided to put my blueprint into action. I knew I needed to make an offer, one that was irresistible, to someone who needed it most. At the time my son was becoming less of a baby and more of a toddler, and it was time to revamp his room. It was also time to revamp our home. I was working from home full-time and when my husband wasn't filming on location, he was also working from home. We were living and working out of our home and things were starting to get claustrophobic. Home remodeling and interior design is in no way my expertise, so I knew I needed to get help. I also knew that I couldn't afford to do what I wanted to do, so I would have to get creative with how to make this happen.

In order to try and build my network base, and to start working with brands at a higher level, I decided to pitch a slew of furniture brands the idea of a room makeover for my son. I googled contacts on press releases, LinkedIn, Twitter—wherever I could find contacts to furniture brands. I just went for it. I pitched about eight different companies my idea, and all of them said no.

The main reason that most of them were saying no was that, at the time, my following and engagement online was not large enough. Basically, they did not see the return on investment. And they were right. I wasn't offering them anything at a fair-trade value. But instead of just giving up, I got curious. *If my reach isn't valuable enough to them*, I wondered, *what is?*

I didn't know the answer. So, I decided to do something that most people never do because most people hate being told "no." Instead of giving up, I chose to remain curious. I asked them what they would find valuable.

That's it. I asked.

Some brands got back to me, and some didn't. Those that did were saying similar things. It all came down to this: the brands wanted media coverage.

So then I started thinking to myself, *Is there a way that I can get media coverage for these brands so I can get what I want?*

That is when I started pitching a different angle. I went back to Google, finding contacts to media outlets in any way I could, and I started pitching them the idea of partnering with me on the bedroom remodel.

Since I was focusing on my son's room and being a mom that worked from home, I went to media outlets that focused on topics like motherhood, children, and parenting.

I was thinking that if I could find one big media outlet or a few smaller ones to cover the story, then maybe the brands would be interested in partnering with me.

I reached out to about a dozen media outlets. Most said no, but then I had one come back. It was the new online section of *People* magazine that featured their coverage on motherhood and blogging.

They shared with me that they were starting to do more home reveals with influencers, bloggers, and tastemakers as their audience really connected with it. They said that if I was able to get a brand to come on board for a before-and-after reveal, they would be interested in discussing this more.

Then, I got even more curious. I wondered, *Well, instead of just getting my son's room remodeled, how can I potentially get my entire house remodeled? Is that possible?*

So, I pitched People.com the idea of doing an entire home before and after remodel. I didn't know if I was going to be able to pull this off, but I knew that I had to at least try to offer something that they would find exclusive, juicy, and irresistible. I was using the angle of a mom who worked from home and a family that was growing in a small space, and how to pull it all together in a way that is organized and functional so you can actually work and live in the same place.

They liked the idea and told me that they would be happy to feature more rooms in the house if I was able to get it all remodeled.

Okay—one step closer. I knew that I had strong interest from a media outlet, and now all I had to do was get a brand on board. So, I went back to the brands I had initially spoken with and told them that People.com was interested in doing a home makeover focusing on moms who work from home.

I was getting closer to perfecting my pitch and now I needed to negotiate—these are two of the most important and life-transforming actions you can take to make your vision a reality.

I took a deep breath and started to type. I told them that in order to get covered by People.com, they would have to remodel multiple rooms in the house, not just one.

Some brands said no, but finally one brand said yes. That brand was World Market. World Market is an incredible company to partner with. They saw the value in real-life stories, in media, and in the new world of bloggers, influencers, and content creation.

Not only was I able to get World Market on board to remodel almost my entire home, but they also threw in free interior design services provided by the company Decorist, which was also looking for media coverage.

And that was it. My pitch met their value. They saw the return on investment, and they decided to invest in me.

The value of this deal, including materials, design services, and media coverage, was more than $250,000! This also created a new wave of influencer partnerships that interior design company Decorist would have for years to come. Decorist saw the value in media coverage and began partnering with other bloggers and influencers on home remodel reveals. This allowed for Decorist to gain national media recognition and helped put their name on the map.

***

What I did was not rocket science.

It wasn't something that had never been done before.

I wasn't special. I just chose to remain curious,

to keep pushing to see what was possible.

I kept asking myself, *What would be their dream come true?* I made this entire pitch about what they wanted first and foremost, not about what I wanted.

It took me about three months from the time that I made my first pitch to the time I actually got this deal secured. Then it took another six months before it all came together. But I stayed consistent, I stayed open-minded, and I kept asking questions and I kept digging. It didn't happen overnight, but it did happen, and it was worth the wait. I was able to repeat this process for years to come, land dozens and dozens of paid sponsorships, make my first six figures, quit my job as a publicist, and go all in on my passion!

This experience was also the catalyst for the creation of my very first online course, Pitch It Perfect. Pitch It Perfect is designed to teach people how to pitch and make money working with brands, getting sponsored to post on social media, and getting featured in the press. I created Pitch It Perfect to take the guesswork out of pitching. Pitch It Perfect works so well because of my experience working alongside the exact brands and outlets people try to pitch every day.

I think the biggest value to this program and why I wanted to share it with the world is my real-life expertise. People want to learn from those who have successfully done what they want to do.

I am always proud to hear when people call this the best pitch program on the market. No other online course on pitching compares to our students' wins, revenue earned, and success rate. By the time people complete the program, they understand who, what, when, and how to pitch effectively. I also teach how much you can charge and how to negotiate for more money.

And now, I want to do the same for you! In this chapter I am going to show you how I pitch. If I can do it, and thousands of my students can do it, you can do it. Once you have the tools and know-how, you, too, will get what you want. I will be walking you through a brief overview of Pitch It Perfect that includes my method. If you want to start seeing results, this is a step you cannot miss or just fly through. And yes, it helps to have reinforcements. I'd love to have you in the Pitch It Perfect community as a wildly successful student, but in the meantime these tools will help you get started so you can begin to pitch, negotiate, and be on your way to seeing amazing changes happen in your life.

But before we get to that, I know some of you may be thinking, *Well, easy for Julie. She's a publicist.* And I get it. Knowing how to use these tools can feel a bit intimidating if you don't feel like you have the background and experience to make it happen. Which is why I must tell you about one of my best friends, pitching guru, author, and life coach Susie Moore. Susie has no background in publicity or journalism. She was born into a very poor home in England and spent most of her early years living in shelters. Susie has gone on to build a beautiful business and life in America. She is a bestselling author and has been covered by all the top media around the world.

When it comes to pitching and landing huge opportunities, Susie says it best.

It simply has four zeros: 0 0 0 0. These represent:

0 college degree

0 writing background

0 media/PR training or experience

0 connections

Yep. You read right. All the things you need—at zero. That's how I got started. Except for the college degree, the rest I gained in action from being featured in the media. It's how you become an expert: gain credibility and authority and create connections. It's in the doing, not the thinking or planning. You don't need what a lot of people assume you need in order to get featured in the biggest media in the world—Oprah, the Today Show, Cosmopolitan, Good Morning America, The Wall Street Journal, CNN, and tons more (I've been in hundreds of media outlets now).

You don't need fancy credentials. You don't need anyone else to approve you. You don't need to be hooked up with the right people. You can do it, wherever you are right now—with what you have! All you need is an idea worth sharing—a story to tell, or something informative, engaging, or helpful to share.

Most people are so much more interesting than they realize. In fact, I've never met a person who wants media coverage who is NOT media worthy. You're ready!

You don't have to have a background in marketing, PR, or anything for that matter to master the skill set and art form that is pitching and negotiating.

Here are what some of the Pitch It Perfect students who also had zero experience pitching before coming into the program had to say:

I took my influencer career full time in January after losing my job, and I just signed a contract for $19,000 for a holiday campaign for a brand!!!! $19,000!!!!!!!!! I couldn't have done anything without PIP and really understanding how the industry works. I have never purchased another course since first joining PIP and the investment has truly returned to me tenfold.

I'm closing the year out making DOUBLE my corporate salary from last year. If this is truly your dream, take this as a sign to keep going!

Tears are rolling down my eyes as I look at this pic. To think last month I was a newbie and 1 month later I've already garnered $8,320 in brand deals. Cheers to beautiful beginnings and way more to come!

I just contracted my highest paid brand deal making June my highest paid month since starting 10 months ago! I'm about $500 away from matching my full time job's monthly salary. Feeling super grateful & excited for the future!

Just wanted to pop in here today to announce that as of this past Friday, I am officially working full time with my wife! We took Pitch it Perfect about a year and a half ago and it has been a crazy whirlwind ever since. From getting brand deals right away in our first month, all the way to being featured on The Influencer Podcast! We are so thankful for this community and all that it has helped us accomplish towards our dreams. I am so thankful I decided to take this course, it has truly made a HUGE difference in my life!

PITCH IT PERFECT

Those of you who have watched my free webinars or have gone through Pitch It Perfect have heard all about pitching. You know this topic like the back of your hand (or should by now), but I still think it's valuable to cover here. It's by no means as in-depth as Pitch It Perfect or working with me personally. But this content is evergreen. It's foundational, and I think everyone can benefit from a refresher. Sometimes reading things, taking notes, and hearing things again makes me realize what I might have missed the first time around. I'm a big believer in reiterating the most important parts of a process, so it really sticks. It's like Zig Ziglar says: "People often say motivation doesn't last. Neither does bathing—that's why we recommend it daily." Sometimes we need to be reminded of what we already know. It's so easy to let things fall by the wayside. Pitching is an activity you will constantly need to hone, practice, and do daily if you intend to master it. I know that, over the years, I've only gotten better with practice.

This may be the first time you've even considered pitching. This may in fact be the first time you've considered monetizing something you truly love to do. You're ready to get what you want, but you just don't know how to take the next steps.

I have good news. You're not alone. I am here to help. I have helped thousands like you walk through this process. And I have better news: your timing couldn't be more perfect. We really are a new generation of leaders because we get to build a following on-line, whether as individuals or as businesses. This has never happened for any generation before us.

Now I don't have to tell you that this opportunity to have a massive impact and reach with the click of a button is truly a gift. The possibilities are endless for us because now, more than at any time before, we have such a low barrier of entry to reach the masses.

BECOMING A PITCH PRO

A Pitch Pro is someone who has high impact and confidence in their work. It's not that they have thousands of clients or a massive following on social media, but it's that there's huge momentum behind what they offer. And they also have a system for securing clients and partnerships consistently that allows them to make real money, which creates massive freedom and the results they've always wanted. A Pitch Pro is someone who commands confidence in the work they do by acting on what they want. And that is what I want for my clients and for you: to be a Pitch Pro.

But I know the journey isn't an easy one. At least it wasn't for me, even with a PR background and a journalism degree. I was shackled by the fear of pitching myself. It was a lot easier for me to pitch clients, but when I had to show up and make it happen for me, I would freeze. I was the living embodiment of the adage "the cobbler's son has no shoes." I was so scared I would get it wrong, or say the wrong thing, or upset someone, or come across as unprofessional, or, worst of all, an impostor. The perfectionism of having to pitch perfect, especially because I was a publicist, held me back for years. But I knew that nothing would change if I kept doing what I was doing. I knew I wanted more, and that meant showing up in a fresh way.

That's when I decided to get above my fear and use a process that I could rely on. And I want the same for you. I want you to know that you're just one pitch away from getting exactly what you want. The revelation I had is that one irresistible pitch can give you the breakthroughs you've been looking for in your brand . . . in such a fast way. I want to share a few ideas that will help you get started today.

Idea 1

The first idea is a mindset strategy you must master. You must understand that pitching is *how you serve*. Now, I'd love to know what you think. What are some of the negative analogies that people use that they associate with pitching? Perhaps sleezy, salesy, or inauthentic comes to mind. Perhaps you start to visualize the used car salesman. These analogies are very common and rooted in our thoughts. And the truth is this: you are already pitching all the time, whether or not you realize it.

You're always pitching something. Think about the words you write in your posts, emails, or website. All you're doing is pitching people on ideas, actions, and values that you desire them to take, and frankly, if we're honest, we're always pitching in our personal lives too.

Think about it. You're pitching your friends and family on what restaurant you want to go to, what book they should read, or what podcast they should listen to. You're pitching them on your perspective, and the values that you believe are important. Make no mistake, you are always pitching something, and that's why pitching is so important in our lives; it's like the air we breathe.

I also want you to think about someone in your life who has made an impact because they pitched you something in some way. Maybe you're reading this book right now because a friend pitched it to you, or I pitched it on my podcast. Maybe you went on a memorable vacation because a loved one or some friends pitched you the idea? Maybe it was an education for your children or education for yourself because you were pitched on the idea of what that education could do for their life or yours?

Now, I want you to imagine if that person decided not to pitch their amazing idea to you because they were scared that someone wouldn't like it, say no, or think it was terrible. I know for me, because I invest in programs and masterminds, I spend a lot of money on my development. I would not have the business I have today if I hadn't invested in programs, coaches, and mastermind groups that were pitched to me by other people.

I wouldn't be married to my husband today if it weren't for pitching. My kids wouldn't exist if it weren't for someone pitching me to go to an event where I met my husband. It's just crazy when you think about it.

Now, this is the kicker. I want you to realize that you are that miracle moment for the people you want to work with. If you don't make a pitch, essentially, you're stealing this opportunity from them.

If you don't give yourself the opportunity to start looking at pitching in a fresh and serving way, everything I'm about to teach you doesn't matter because there will be too much resistance in you to make pitches.

In fact, could you write this down? *Pitching is the start of a game-changing transformation.* I want you to write that down because I want you to remember it. Put it somewhere you can see it every day. If you started to believe pitching is truly a service, what would that enable you to do? What's the first feeling that comes to mind? And, most important, can you commit to making that shift in your mind today?

Idea 2

The next idea is that you need a signature pitch. Most people make this mistake that they think they talk about themselves when they pitch. Your signature pitch has nothing to do with you.

Your signature pitch is the journey the prospect needs to experience the value you're promising them by working together. You represent what they want.

Talking about yourself is very general; everyone can do that. But a signature pitch is a specific opportunity that transfers a belief that the brand must have to say yes to you. I want to say that again, a signature pitch that converts is a specific opportunity that transfers a belief that the brand must have to say yes to you. And the reason why this is so powerful is that signature pitches transfer connection.

They transfer beliefs. And they reduce the resistance that someone could have; really, our ego holds up, especially in a sales environment when you're trying to get a brand to work with you.

What a signature pitch does is it brings forth that part of us that craves connection and authentic relationships. The reason why signature pitches are so powerful is that when you share the right pitch, it sells what you want without selling.

If you create and share your signature pitch correctly, what will happen is your prospect will go, *Oh my gosh, what she's offering is exactly what we're looking for. I am so relating to her right now.* And people want to work with people they relate to.

That's why you create a signature pitch, not so that people will like you or think that you're amazing. It's so that prospects can emotionally engage and see that you're able to deliver what they desire most.

There are three elements involved in a signature pitch. The first element is connection. Your pitch should share a connection because people will relate to authenticity more than success. The success inspires them, but they relate to authenticity.

The second element is credibility. And, in fact, credibility is normally less grand than you realize. The credibility can be a result you experienced or a breakthrough you had. It could be an award or accreditation you received. It could be the results you have. It could be the people or other companies you worked with.

And then the final element is the pitch promise. And this is the secret sauce that not many people teach. The pitch promise is the one idea that if your prospect believes that idea, then working with you would make sense.

For me, typically, marketing, coaching, or something education or self-development related will be the pitch promise. I have a client who is a sleep coach for babies. Her pitch promise is sleep training.

Maybe you think you don't have anything to promise? Don't believe that for a second! We all do; you just must get creative. For example, I had the opportunity recently to work with a content creator named Kassie. Her pitch promise is her curly hair. That's it! Using her curly hair as her pitch promise, she monetizes her platform and grows her community. She was recently on every end cap in ULTA stores across the country and got paid a very lucrative deal with a curly hair product company. Just the hair on her head brought her that fantastic opportunity.

Idea 3

You need to follow a formula. If you look at all the best content creators, marketers, and influencers, they've got frameworks they follow.

I'm not very good at winging things—for example, baking. I wanted to bake this cake that my mom makes, so I called her and asked, "Can you send me the recipe?" She said, "Oh, you just get some butter and lots of sugar and flour and bake it until it gets bubbly." I thought to myself: "Okay, but how much is some butter? How much is a lot of sugar? Lots to you may be different than lots to me."

And so, I could grab all the ingredients and hope for the best. But I don't even know what I'm doing. And I doubt it's going to taste good. And that's what a lot of people do with their pitches.

They go, "I'm just going to grab it all and just hope for the best." Or, really smart people do this. Instead, they say, "I can get one of the pre-made recipes, follow the instructions, and maybe add something that I like, chocolate or cinnamon." And suddenly, the cake is pretty good. It tastes amazing. And so that's what I mean about having a formula—they are a critical factor in getting the best result faster and easier.

I want to share a bit about my formula now. There are three pitches you need to master, the Sharp Pitch, the Soft Pitch, and the No Pitch. I can't lay out all the processes in detail in this book, but I do want to go over the Sharp Pitch.

THE SHARP PITCH METHOD

There are three elements to the Sharp Pitch. The first piece is to connect. Remember, prospects that you want to work with are human beings. So, act human. And what I mean by that is this is where you emotionally engage people in the content so that they go: "Wow, this feels good, it feels right. I want to work with this person."

The second piece is the content in the pitch. This is where you start to shift their thinking. You don't teach something or give many details; you shift their thinking. The goal here is to shift people's minds so that they are ready to make a greater commitment in the area that you can help them with.

And the final piece is the close. You get them to say yes! The flow to start practicing is this. You motivate them in. You connect with them. You get them hooked into the pitch promise you have. You shift their thinking. Then you transition into your offer. Finally, you close the deal.

PITCH TEMPLATES TO GET YOU STARTED

In my Pitch It Perfect program, I have more than thirty-five pitch templates that cover any pitching situation you can imagine. I also offer my students monthly audits, where I personally review and edit their pitches, so they are equipped with feedback in real time. I want to share two of my favorite ones with you. You can get started with pitching today by using these.

Hi X,

My name is [INSERT YOUR NAME], and I'm such a fan of [PRODUCT/ COMPANY/ BRAND].

I've been an avid [FAN, CONSUMER, LISTENER, READER] for X years and love what you're creating with [INSERT SPECIFIC PROJECT, PRODUCT, OR WORK OF THEIRS].

I appreciate what you said about [INSERT A SPECIFIC IDEA, TEACHING, OR CONCEPT YOU'VE LEARNED FROM THEM OR ADMIRE ABOUT WHAT THEY DO].

Hi X,

Hope you are doing great! I enjoyed your story on [MENTION A RECENT STORY THEY DID THAT YOU WATCHED OR READ]. In fact, I just downloaded the X that you recommended—great stuff!

Let me introduce myself; I'm X, [INSERT ELEVATOR PITCH HERE].

I think I'd be an excellent resource for future stories on [X OUTLET] and would love for you to keep me in mind for expert contributing opportunities.

Some of my specific story ideas include:

[COULD BE A MUST-HAVE, HOW-TO, OR ANY TIPS OR TRICKS YOU HAVE LEARNED THAT ARE UNIQUE AND HELPFUL TO THEIR READERS]

1. [PROPOSED TITLE OR TOPIC—SUMMARY OF CONTENT]
2. [PROPOSED TITLE OR TOPIC—SUMMARY OF CONTENT]
3. [PROPOSED TITLE OR TOPIC—SUMMARY OF CONTENT]

I'm also equipped to weigh in on [WHATEVER YOUR EXPERTISE IS, SUCH AS FASHION TRENDS, BEAUTY MUST-HAVES, OR HEALTH TOPICS].

My bio and website are below. Thanks so much for considering these stories, and I look forward to connecting and working with you soon.

Best,

X

[QUICK BIO WITH LINK TO WEBSITE AND SOCIALS]

YOUR TURN

Use one of these templates to Pitch It Perfect!

If you want more support, I'd love for you to join my free webinar! You can sign up at pitchitperfect.net/webinar.

CHAPTER EIGHT

How to Negotiate to Get What You Want

Once you learn how to Pitch It Perfect, you're going to start getting offers. But before you get too excited and jump at the opportunity to take the money coming your way, I want you to know that there is an option available to you: negotiation.

Most women I know have been taught to be pleasing, courteous, grateful, and "happy with what they've got." And so they are terrified of asking for what they really want.

But here's the thing: negotiation is everywhere. Our daily professional and personal lives are riddled with negotiations—on a computer screen, across the kitchen table, and everywhere in between. Love it or hate it, you have to master the art of negotiation.

Knowing how to negotiate is a superpower. It can literally transform a bad deal into an amazing deal that works for everyone—most especially you.

Whether you are an entrepreneur trying to raise money, or an employee trying to convince your boss, or a parent trying to persuade your kid, I'm going to show you how to negotiate more effectively.

Negotiation is an open process for two parties to find an acceptable solution for an opportunity they wish to achieve. Whether you're negotiating a multimillion-dollar contract or simply which restaurant to meet for dinner, it's important to set the stage for a negotiation to take place in a productive and mutually beneficial manner so you can achieve your desired result.

By "setting the stage" I mean that you must prepare so that positive and productive negotiations can take place.

There are three opportunities I have found to be extremely beneficial when setting a negotiation stage.

OPPORTUNITY 1:
GIVE A SINCERE COMPLIMENT

When setting the stage for a negotiation, give your prospect a genuine compliment. Let them know that you admire their work. You love their products. You think their service is fantastic.

Complimenting a person or company not only makes them feel good about their offer but it also makes you ask yourself what it is you really admire and like about them. It helps you align your goal to their offer. It allows for compassion and excitement about their services to come to fruition for you, which leads to more genuine support.

OPPORTUNITY 2:
GET CURIOUS

Questions are the secret to winning a negotiation. So ask your prospect thoughtful and results-driven questions such as:

- What are your goals for the year?
- What new offers or opportunities do you have coming out that you are most excited about?
- What are your biggest challenges when it comes to XYZ?
- How important is it to you to find a solution for this challenge?
- What hasn't worked for you in the past and why?
- How can I support your goals?

These are just a few questions to get your own creative juices flowing, which I've also included at the end of this chapter. Feel free to write these down and use them yourself, but remember, you are your own boss. You have your own ideas, thoughts, creative angles, and goals. Ask the questions you need answered that will help you offer support and service.

OPPORTUNITY 3:
GIVE THE RELATIONSHIP TIME TO BUILD

Everyone knows that relationships are key in business, so give yourself time to build them. They are the foundation of loyalty, trust, and respect between you and the prospect. Plus, people genuinely like working with those with whom they have good relationships.

But relationships are not built overnight. If that is your expectation when trying to collaborate, you are going to be disappointed.

You have to be realistic with yourself that building relationships takes time, as does mastering the art of negotiation.

In my opinion, developing relationships is just as important as monetization, if not more. It's what leads to long-term growth.

A great tip for building relationships is to go beyond the email. Ask the person you're pitching to coffee or lunch if you live close. If not, a virtual session works too. Share your time with them. Make sure that you treat them to lunch if they let you. Do what you can to make them feel important and special. I promise it pays off!

Now let's talk about how to become more comfortable with negotiating. Because I get it. Negotiating anything can be terrifying. But when you get to the root of negotiating, it can be a lot easier to practice and perfect over time.

There are many situations in a collaboration that can call for you to negotiate. Some of them are small negotiations that do not require much thought and you may not even notice you are negotiating. At the other end are situations that require a lot of preparation and probably cause you a good deal of anxiety. All of these negotiations have at least one thing in common: they are governed by societal rules of what you "should" or "should not" do.

Now, these rules are created over the years based on our own cultural norms and values. By culture I mean the culture within which you were raised, as well as the culture of our industry. These rules govern your relationships and affect what you should or should not say, or should or should not ask for, in your negotiations.

Negotiation goes hand in hand with your mindset and beliefs.

It is always good to consider both the process and the outcomes of your negotiations, because relationships need to be nurtured on both fronts.

What I'm about to walk you through has a lot to do with your own psychology and mindset, so if you don't get this at first, that is okay. Just don't give up. Give yourself time and patience with this. Mindsets and beliefs don't change overnight.

First, it's important to understand that a lot of people think they will fail at negotiating, or that they don't know how to negotiate and are not capable of figuring it out. This thought pattern comes from limiting beliefs around how we "should" communicate and behave around other people. It's a disease to please.

No one wants to come off as naggy, overbearing, silly, or stupid. So we choose not to negotiate. Instead, we just accept whatever is offered. We settle. And by doing this, we become powerless to our own dreams, goals, and freedom.

You will not get negotiations right every time, but that's not the goal. The goal is to notice what is holding you back and to gain the courage to negotiate even if you can't predict or control the outcome.

If you think about pitching, negotiation, and influence in a fresh way, you can be extraordinarily effective and do something really important for the world, other people, and ultimately yourself!

THE THREE-STEP NEGOTIATION STRATEGY SYSTEM

After setting the negotiation stage, it's time to put a tried-and-true system in place to get what you want in the negotiation.

Step 1: Getting Ready to Negotiate— Self-Reflection Questions

It all starts with asking yourself these important questions so you are clear on your goals and how to best achieve them.

1. What is my goal with this negotiation?
2. How much time will this take to produce success and quality results?
3. What services or resources will I need to provide quality results?
4. How does this negotiation help grow my brand, business, or ability to carry out my vision?
5. What business goals does this impact short term? Long term?
6. Is this negotiation mutually beneficial? If not, how can I make it so?

By simply engaging in a problem-solving negotiation, you have become a partner in the solution, and a willing and able resource in the prospect's problem-solving process.

In a best-case scenario, you've made yourself an indispensable partner in fulfilling the prospect's needs, their requirements, and your goals at the same time.

Step 2: Setting the Stage— Your "Get Curious" Questions

Once negotiations are in place, you want to make sure that you have everything the prospect is asking of you, and that you have it in writing. This is where scope of work, expectations, time frame, goals, and objectives are asked and clearly defined. Just as important as your questions were in setting the stage, these are important for presenting your offer.

1. So I know how to best be of service, can you share with me your goals?
2. What is the scope of work?

3. Are there important stats, processes, or procedures I need to be aware of to better provide results for you?
4. What is the approval process like on your end?
5. Do you have a deadline in mind to reach this goal?
6. Is there important branding or messaging I need to be aware of?
7. Do you have examples of previous achieved goals or successful collaborations that you can share?

Step 3: Present Your Negotiation

Once you have gone through Steps 1 and 2, you can formally present your offer and confirm the opportunity based on the information you have gathered and what you are willing (or not willing) to do.

Remember to give yourself permission to omit or change anything you are not comfortable with. You want to make this a realistic and attainable win for you and the prospect. Make sure you are setting yourself up for success. Don't agree to asks, goals, or budgets that you don't think you can achieve.

The reason why someone doesn't invest in something isn't because it's too expensive, but because they don't see the value in it. If you want to make more money, create more value!

Lastly, when you are negotiating, remember to focus on value, not money. It's not about the money. Really. It's about the value you provide; it's about how working with you will make their lives easier and their businesses richer.

Help them imagine how much better their business and life would be working with you.

I want to remind you that the art of negotiating will look and feel different for everyone. The Negotiation Questions Cheat Sheet offers you a quick recap and an easy way to find the most important questions. It can be modified to suit your needs, depending on your situation.

The questions are placed in the order that I like to follow for ease and clarity, but you can change it up if you want. For example, you may find that you want to get curious with your prospect before you ask yourself reflection questions. If that feels better for you, then do that.

No matter what order you choose, make sure that you take some time with each series of questions.

I don't advise asking yourself your set of questions while simultaneously asking the prospect questions. That can result in too much information, which could overwhelm and confuse both you and your prospect. The goal here is to have a clear focus on what you want and how to get it.

With clarity in mind, the cheat sheet is a jumping-off point for brainstorming more questions, so feel free to let those thoughts and ideas run at the bottom of the "Your Turn" section.

NEGOTIATION QUESTIONS CHEAT SHEET

Keep a copy of this somewhere you can easily reference when you're on the phone or near your computer.

Getting Ready to Negotiate
Self-Reflection Questions

- What is my goal with this negotiation?
- How much time will this take to produce success and quality results?
- What services or resources will I need to provide quality results?
- How does this negotiation help grow my brand, business, or ability to carry out my vision?
- What business goals does this impact short term? Long term?
- Is this negotiation mutually beneficial? If not, how can I make it so?

Setting the Stage
Your "Get Curious" Questions

- So I know how to best be of service, can you share with me your goals?
- What is the scope of work?
- Are there important stats, processes, or procedures I need to be aware of to better provide results for you?
- What is the approval process like on your end?
- Do you have a deadline in mind to reach this goal?
- Is there important branding or messaging I need to be aware of?
- Do you have examples of previous achieved goals or successful collaborations that you can share?

YOUR TURN

What other questions do you plan on asking the prospect or yourself to make sure your negotiation is a success? Add them here!

_____

_____

_____

PART THREE

The Results

CHAPTER NINE

Limitless

A couple of years ago, life was on a smooth track. My husband, John, and I were renovating a house we had purchased, when we found out we were pregnant with our second child.

John and I thought it would be a good idea to refinance our home. We called our lender and set the wheels in motion.

A few weeks later I got a call from our lender. He told me that our refinancing approval was on hold because I needed more credit.

Needed more credit?

I didn't understand. I had a thriving business and I consistently made a great income every single month. I had worked for years to become debt free and to pay all my bills on time. The lender clarified that my credit wasn't bad, there just wasn't enough of it.

Most of my credit was from my business. But I, Julie Solomon, did not have enough credit to refinance a home. I was one point away from where we needed to be.

I couldn't believe what I was hearing. I felt defeated, embarrassed, and ashamed. How could I have missed this? What have I been doing these past few years? I thought I had gotten so responsible and proactive about my finances and now I'm having someone remind me that, yet again, I'm a financial toddler. Due to my previous years of being so reckless with money, I had scared myself to death over having a credit card. I would hear the voices of financial gurus like Dave Ramsey in my head tell me how awful a credit card is and if you needed a credit card for something then you couldn't afford it. With the fear of history repeating itself, I had made a promise to myself that I would never get myself in that situation again. Therefore, I never used a personal credit card. I would always use a debit card, which I thought was safe. I thought that was the right thing to do. And maybe it was, to a degree. Little did I know, it was keeping me from growing the credit we needed to refinance our home.

My old origin story and everything I had been told to believe about finances started flooding into my body. Clearly, for this to come back up, there was a pattern that still hadn't been broken. Had the pendulum swung so far to the other side that I put myself in another risky financial situation?

That's the thing with growth and success:

it's truly a lifelong journey.

Even when we reach success, hit milestones,

and see results, the work is not done.

Once I had the awareness of my reality and accepted what it was, I was able to take action. I signed up for Experian Boost and began finding ways through their paid service to boost my credit.

I also applied for a personal credit card and started paying for things like groceries, post office runs, and drugstore purchases each week. And each month I would pay off the credit card in full. Doing so helped with raising my credit score by six points in just a month. It seemed like a quick and easy fix, but I couldn't shake off the feeling of ignorance and shame that loomed from not having a stronger credit score to begin with.

I began to chat with family members about what happened and realized most of the women in my family didn't have a lot of personal credit either. It turned out their husbands handled all things financial, so they never had a reason to worry much about it. I asked women in my community about their credit. Some proudly shared how they had worked hard to build amazing credit. Others shared how they had hit some hard roads and were working their way out of bad credit. Some women were like deer caught in the headlights when it came to the conversation. They had never really thought about their credit score or the need to worry about it. Some of the women I talked to told me they had no idea what their credit score was.

As I sat at the dining room table updating John on my credit fiasco, we talked about this idea around credit. John found it so interesting that I wasn't raised to learn about the importance of building personal credit. He kept reminding me that strong credit was something that his father hammered into his head since he was a young boy. It was vital that he not only have credit, but that his credit was excellent.

However, as we were having this conversation, my husband realized that his own mother didn't own a credit card herself. She never needed to because her husband, his father, handled all of that. My husband, like me, did not come from a wealthy family.

Rich or poor, it didn't seem to matter. He knew the importance of this. So why had I been left out of the credit conversation? Why is it that at age thirty-five I was still dealing with issues around financial literacy?

I started to talk to some of my friends in heterosexual relationships and noticed the common mindset around this idea. It generally goes like this: most men want to be the ones who take care of everything financially, so they're going to spend their time and energy building credit and wealth for the family. Because of this, the woman's credit and finances are not much of a factor. What I also found interesting was my friends in same sex marriages said this wasn't as much of an issue in their relationships.

The questions that I had pondered for years started flooding back in. Why is it assumed by the culture I was raised in that women's finances aren't as important as their husbands'? Why is it assumed that all of this is going to be handled for us and taken care of by a man? Why is it assumed that half of the population need not worry about being financially literate and independent?

I know this isn't the case for all women. Many are the breadwinners of their households. A lot of women are single mothers and must do it all on their own. Yet, in the culture I grew up in, there is still this social belief that financial independence and wealth is an obligation for a man and a choice for a woman.

Credit cards aren't bad. Misusing them is. And even though I knew this conceptually, why was I letting a myth about women, men, and money get in the way of me being 100 percent responsible for myself? What if my husband gets hit by a bus tomorrow? What the hell am I supposed to do?

The answer is: I have to be prepared. There is nothing to do after the tragedy strikes or the divorce happens or the unexpected occurs. No one ever thinks it will happen to them until it does. I know too many stories of women who handed over the finances to the man of the house or disregarded their own personal finances because they didn't think they were worthy or prepared to do it, and ended up losing everything they had worked so hard to achieve.

Many people think that once they become rich or achieve the "magic number" in their head, their work is done. The reality is much more brutal. You need to have the proper mindset and skill set. If you're not prepared to handle money and success, you can easily lose it.

BELIEVING IN YOUR SUCCESS AND EARNING POTENTIAL IS LIMITLESS

One of my clients, Amy, now makes $3 million a year as a coach in the styling industry. When she came to me she was working as a hairstylist and earning around $45,000 a year. Amy had to overcome a lot to get where she is today, not the least of which were the old stories about money passed on to her by her family. Amy had no college degree, no dreams, and zero expectations. When I asked her what she was taught about money as a child, she, with a pitch-perfect Michigan accent, revealed, "My mom told me thousands of times that she didn't want me to end up like her, which was no degree and barely getting by. College would be the answer to it all. The normal path for me was just not to have to be broke and to do something that afforded me to pay my bills without worry. That was about it. I was never taught that I could dream big, or that I could be the absolute best at what I do."

When I read this, it made me sad for that little girl. I imagined going back in time to when she was in second grade and sharing with her all the possibilities for her life. I wanted that little girl to know that the opportunity to be who she wants to be, and to make as much money as she wants, is not an opportunity that was given so easily to women who came before her.

I want everyone to know this. I want you to know it. The opportunity laid out before you is limitless.

You don't have to follow a path that requires you to compromise. There is no financial hierarchy unless you actively participate in creating one.

When my clients were younger, I didn't have the opportunity to support them, but now I do. As soon as I begin working with a client, I insist that they think about themselves, their beliefs, and their thoughts differently. Oftentimes, I push them out of their own resistance spins and limiting beliefs to drown out messages that they can't do it, that they don't know how, or that they aren't capable. I always encourage them to give themselves a bigger chance.

Fortunately, many of my clients have courageously believed me. They decided to test out my method, and in doing so they have achieved greatness. They have created iconic success, success that defies the rules and expectations of most people today.

The biggest compliment I ever receive from clients is, "You gave me the confidence and clarity to push myself, and because of that I have literally changed my entire life!"

But I can't help thinking: What if they had believed that sooner? What if, when these women were girls, we didn't limit their potential? What if we told them that being something new and unique would be their secret to success? What if we told them that they didn't need permission to listen to that still, small voice inside them that was only getting louder? What if we told them that you find answers by trying, failing, and learning? What if they discovered that failure is a vital part of success?

What if we gave girls bigger *what-ifs*?

What if we told girls they could be amazing wives and mothers, or not if they chose? What if we told them they could work for themselves, or for a company that values their talents and recognizes their greatness? What if girls believed that making as much money as they desired was a laudable and achievable goal, if that's what they want? If girls knew that financial independence makes it easy to say no to a spouse who isn't respectful, a power player who is manipulating them, or a problem that they do not have time or energy to solve, how would it influence their decisions?

What if girls knew that *no* is a complete sentence and explaining yourself wasn't necessary or needed? What if girls knew that being wealthy and free was part of their destiny? This should never cause them to feel guilty, but rather motivate them. What if girls believed that the freedom to earn as much money as they want is a gift, not a burden?

The truth is money does grow on trees,

and they just keep making more of it.

So, you either claim it or you don't.

My mom always told me the chances of you selling yourself out for money are much higher when you don't have any. Money is nothing more than an exchange of energy. It gives you the privilege to make choices that align with who you most want to be. Most important, it gives you freedom.

American systems scientist and bestselling author Peter Senge says that people do one of two things. They will either have a vision and change their reality to achieve the vision; or they will lower that vision to accommodate a comfortable reality.

Which one will you choose?

The world might try to pull you into some version of realistic thinking, so that you don't get your hopes up or remember what really matters. Don't fall for any of this. You have to know that you are the creator of your life and your own possibility.

It's time you suit up and show up because the most limiting thing we can do is play it safe.

You don't have to ask anyone for permission to be more successful. It's allowed. I've already asked all those people you think you need permission from, and they said, "Yup, this life is yours for the taking, see if you can get what you want."

"I'M NOT GOOD WITH NUMBERS," AND OTHER NONSENSE WE BELIEVE

Recently, I was scrolling through Instagram and I landed on a page of an influencer I follow. She was polling her followers with "get to know me" questions and one came up that caught my attention. Over 85 percent of her 883,000 followers that participated (all female by the way) voted for "I don't like numbers/math." She went on to explain how she was just like them. She also didn't like math and hated numbers and didn't really care about money, all while giving her followers a walk-through of her brand-new, $4 million home and raking in money every day from selling clothes through her affiliate links.

I couldn't stop thinking about these opposing ideas. Here she was, living this extremely full, beautiful, and rich life. A life that a lot of money had made happen. But she didn't like numbers or care about money?

I sat there frozen, thinking to myself, *Wow, these influential women online, with hundreds of thousands of followers, with believers and other women that look to them daily for inspiration and encouragement are just sitting here and saying, "Well, I'm not good with numbers. That isn't for me; I don't care about the money," so casually as if someone had asked them if they liked oat milk in their coffee.*

But that doesn't make any sense. Money is a tool that's meant to be used, just like we need a key to open a lock, or a hammer to put a nail in the wall.

When I was growing up, my parents had to care about money. They didn't have a lot of it, which is why caring was so important.

My mom always says, "If you can say 'I don't care about money' then you've truly never gone without it." Ask anyone who has ever lived paycheck to paycheck. Ask a mother who works three jobs to make sure her kids have shoes on their feet. Ask a child who had to start working at age nine to help pay their family's bills, like my father had to, if they care about the money. I promise you they will all say yes.

Not caring about money is a privilege. Because when you *do* go without, you know the power money has to change your life. It affects all your basic needs—shelter, food, access, healthcare, you name it. Caring about money matters a lot.

To say it doesn't matter is insulting to those who work hard for it or who truly don't have it. They don't have the luxury not to care.

Do most women see a connection about the omission, denial, and shame they have around caring about money and what that does to our thoughts about money?

When I hear women saying they don't care, what I notice is that they don't like to admit that they don't understand. Because they don't believe that it's possible for them to be responsible for, and capable of, making as much money as they want.

It's how we are socialized. We are trained to believe that talking about money is tacky and caring about money means you're being greedy, or bad-mannered. And I'll tell you, that belief is literally what's keeping you stuck right now.

Let's be real. Yes, you care about money. And you need to care about money, especially if you're an adult, a parent, a caregiver, or a business owner. Money matters. You need to care *for* it. You need to care *about* it.

And if you're running or working for a business, you need to care a lot about money. A business is defined as a company that makes a profit. That's the goal of a business. So, if you truly don't care about money, then don't work for a business, don't start a business, don't build a brand.

HERE IS YOUR PERMISSION SLIP
FOR UNLIMITED MONEY

I also think saying "I don't care about money" is part of a lot of women's desire to please people. A lot of women say this because they want to be clear that they don't care about money more than other things in their life. Notice I'm not talking about *spending* money here. I'm talking about *using* money, which means safety, security, helping others, and opening doors that would otherwise be closed to you.

Money is meant to be used.

I want to give everyone permission to care enough about your money. Caring is the first step. You don't have to love money at the expense of something else more important than money.

And, most important, can we all sign a metaphorical contract that caring about money doesn't mean that you care about money more than you care about other important people and things in your life?

That's not the case with the most successful people I know. For them, it's always about the people and service first. Always.

In fact, the more you take care of people, the more you honor your customer, the more you look out for those around you whom you love, the more money you will make. That's how abundance and gratitude works.

A few years ago I started saying a mantra to myself over and over again. The mantra is, "I love money." I know some of you freak out just reading that. But it's true. I do love money. When I say that, I feel this sense of connection and abundance and generosity with it. It's very powerful. It took me years to be confident, both mentally and emotionally, to say those words out loud and actually mean it.

If you want to experience more abundance, you're going to have to change your relationship with money.

So, practice saying out loud, "I care about money. I want to make more money. I love money. *Show me the money!*"

If it seems impossible for you to say that today, then give yourself the permission to work toward that.

Think about who would be attracted to you if you said, "I love money. I care for money. I want money," instead of, "I'm not interested in it. It's not important. That's not my focus."

It's true, money can't buy you happiness,

but neither can poverty or a heaping mound of

debt—and money is a heck of a lot more stable,

secure, and fun. You can either love it or hate it.

What's your choice?

I have to say that my relationship with money has changed my relationship with myself. And I'm reminded every day that my relationship with money is directly affected by my relationship with my clients, my community, and you.

And that's why I honor the work that I've done. It is, I think, a reflection of me caring about myself enough to care about money and my ability to use it to get what I want and give it in service of others. I want to invite you to do the same.

Notice even the little things that you say about money; write them down. I want you to start talking about money the way that you would talk about a child you love. I want you to think of money as something that can have its feelings hurt. What are you saying about it? Would it like what it is hearing?

Money opens a lot of doors and can give you access and limitless possibilities. Don't be ashamed, be grateful. And find other people with like minds who share your deep respect and gratitude for it.

YOUR TURN

Imagine a scenario beyond your wildest dreams. What does it look like? What does it feel like? What could you do with all that money, time, freedom, and resources? What could you have? What could you build? What would you use your money to create or help with? Who and what could benefit from all the money you make? Write that down here:

_____

_____

_____

If you have money right now and it's already exceeded your wildest dreams, can you expand that dream? Can you imagine having even more? Doing more? What would that look like? Write that down here:

_____

_____

_____

If you're currently avoiding "dealing with money," what can you do today to change course? Do you have your own credit card? Have you checked your credit lately? Your bank statements? Do you regularly check in on your financial goals or talk about them with your significant other or spouse? If not, what needs to change? Give yourself an honest assessment of your financial health and well-being here:

_____

_____

_____

CHAPTER TEN

The Importance
of Masterminds

I think one thing people don't realize about me is that I am an
introvert. And as I have gotten older, my introversion has
gotten bolder. I loathe *working the room* or, even worse, social-
izing with strangers. Now, you can throw me on a stage or a live
masterclass with thousands of people in attendance, and sure, I'll
be a little nervous, but I will kill it—every time. But the minute
you ask me to do something like happy hour with a bunch of people I don't know, I'll immediately want to curl up in the fetal position and die. I have lived with myself long enough to know that if
I force myself into something like that, I may end up being so quiet
that I could come off as supercilious or aloof when really, I'm just
more reserved than most would think.

That is why masterminds have been a godsend for people like
me. Support and connection through Zoom calls or intimate,

in-person retreats are less intimidating and decentralized than the conference ballroom filled with rows of people wearing name tags or the local after-work pub where getting beer sloshed all over you is a requirement for entry.

I am braver and more at ease in a mastermind setting. As a result, I've learned to build honest relationships and network in a way that feels a little more comfortable and truer to me, which is why masterminds have been so crucial in my growth and business. I just wish I had found them sooner.

If I could go back to the beginning of my business and do only one thing, I would join a mastermind. A mastermind is a peer-to-peer mentoring and networking group used to help members create more impact and growth in their business. Typically, this is done with input and advice from the other group members, along with the leader of the mastermind and their network of experts, influencers, and strategists. The concept was coined in 1925 by author Napoleon Hill in his book *The Law of Success* and described in more detail in his 1937 book, *Think and Grow Rich*. If you're not part of a mastermind right now, then you're going to want to look for one. It could be one in your community, city, or region; or it could be a national one.

The one thing that has transformed my business the most is, without a doubt, masterminds. Whether I was growing and scaling, creating multiple products, selling millions of dollars in courses, dissolving services that didn't fit well, launching a podcast, speaking on stages, or pitching and landing this book deal, masterminds were the key for the brand, exposure, impact, and revenue growth I created.

I knew very early in my journey that proximity to mentors, as well as experts in my industry with whom I aligned and built relationships, was pivotal in taking me to the next level. These relationships helped me gain access to resources and leverage connections so that I was in close proximity to other influential people in my space, particularly those who had already created what I wanted to create. Gaining access to and surrounding myself with the right people was way more beneficial than strategies and tips.

This is the best business advice I could ever give someone: if you want to be successful, you need to join a mastermind.

Bottom line: access to this type of group is one of the most powerful things that you can have in your toolkit to grow your business or change your life.

Now, why should you be looking for a mastermind in the first place? Some of you may even think, *Is it right for me? Am I ready for one?* When I started out I was constantly traveling to different industry conferences. I was going to industry events where I met influencers, leaders, and experts who had connections and information that I wanted. I was building brand partners through these professionals and peers in different industries. It was extremely powerful having access to the right people and being able to text or call someone for feedback or advice. However, I went as far as I could with this. I was looking to accelerate this process and couldn't see to it on my own. I had done the courses, conferences, and workshops. I had gotten the free support and the brand deals. But I hit a wall. I knew that in order to scale my vision to that next phase I needed a community that worked from a deeper level of support with one another. One that would not only teach me things I didn't know businesswise but, more important, would introduce me to people I could partner with and leverage when it came to my own success, and vice versa.

What I really wanted was to hit seven figures in revenue and meet people who would truly make a difference in my life and business. So, in sum, the main reasons I joined my first mastermind were to get what I wanted: financial growth, impact, recognition, and freedom.

In 2017, an opportunity came through my inbox from an entrepreneur whose email list I was on, and I applied. I got on a call with the team and was accepted. I invested in my very first mastermind. It was $25,000 for a year of enrollment.

I'd never invested that kind of money in myself ever, and yes, it was absolutely terrifying. It was almost the cost of a four-year college degree. But I also knew I needed to be a part of a community that was thinking and working at a higher level and was on the trajectory I wanted to be on. So it goes back to the question of who I needed to be—not what things I needed to have—in order to get what I wanted.

I knew I had to trust a process that was greater than my own understanding. I signed up for the $25,000 payment plan. In that year, because I chose to self-select into a mastermind and be surrounded by a new level of support, I went from $250,000 to $1.3 million. I also spoke on stages in front of more than forty thousand people. My podcast grew tenfold. I became known as one of the best in my industry. All because I chose to invest in myself and trusted the process of a mastermind, even though I was scared.

This is why I love masterminds so much: because of the insane impact it can have on your business. There's such an amazing feeling when you are surrounded by other people who are also on that same path. There is no greater feeling than going through challenging times and coming out on the other side even more successful than you were before. Masterminds taught me one of the best business lessons: growth is an investment, not an expense.

Masterminds also give you access to connections that you would never have otherwise, which are so important. The group that you surround yourself with matters. Your container matters. Whether it's your friend group, Facebook groups, or groups that you pay to be in, they can show you if you are on the path to success or not. Mastermind groups, in my opinion, are the best of the best.

Now, once I was in, I didn't know what all to expect. I was so nervous when I went to my first mastermind gathering. But that quickly changed. They discussed things I had never heard of before that were transformative for me. It just blew my mind wide open. There were probably six or seven things during the first couple of calls together that helped me double my revenue that first month.

Over the course of the next month, I had built four key relationships out of this mastermind. They wanted to promote my work and, best of all, they wanted to invest in my work. I wanted to invest in theirs too. We became one another's colleagues, clients, and experts. Most important, we became very close friends. We even started to travel together outside of the mastermind group.

One of the women, Liz, called me up recently. "I just went through your webinar," she said. "It's great, but I noticed these three things you might want to consider changing . . ." It will probably mean that I will be making thousands more from my webinar. She didn't have to do that, but she *wanted* to do that. It's just what we do with each other.

That's why I say relationships are everything and why a mastermind is so transformative. It's the people you meet and how you end up supporting one another for the rest of your life.

I also learned countless ways to optimize my business and how to save time, money, and accelerate growth that I implemented. All of this did something else for me: it created a sense of accountability at a level I've never faced before. There I was in a roomful of peers I highly respected, with a facilitator guiding all of us. It made me level up the way I thought, the way I acted, and the way I believed in myself more than I ever had before. That's when I realized I need to be a part of masterminds throughout my career. It was going to be part of my business investment just like renting office space or buying a laptop or hiring an assistant. That's when I also realized I needed to create and facilitate my own mastermind. After years of experiencing the lack of a solid network that supports leaders at a higher level, I created a mastermind. SHINE is a premier network mastermind and program for leaders who are ready to accelerate their impact, grow their influential network, and create iconic success. SHINE is different from other opportunities. We make sure members connect with other vetted high-level peers along with my own vast network of experts, tastemakers, and industry leaders. This allows members who are willing to tap into valuable relationships and resources that can help grow their brand, status, and ventures. SHINE members are credible leaders in their fields, but they come to me because they are missing that next-level influence and impact piece. SHINE supports them in getting there. What I love most about my SHINE mastermind is that it's an exclusive network that you can't find anywhere else. I didn't want it to be just another strategy-based container. I wanted to create something that promised high-level support through relationships, exposure, and brand recognition. This is why figuring out what kind of mastermind is best for you is so important.

TIPS FOR JOINING A MASTERMIND

Here are some things to look for when joining a mastermind:

- *The mastermind leader needs to be extremely credible and connected.* If you want to succeed, you must learn from someone who has actually done what you want to do and has the network and connections to people you want access to. I firmly believe that is a big key to success. The mastermind leader needs to be someone who has accomplished what you're trying to accomplish. They need to be someone who has created results that you want, and someone that can connect you with people who can help you achieve your next level of success. It doesn't mean you have to be them; it doesn't mean you have to copy them; it just means you aspire to learn from them, and they must have credibility in their industry to get you access to a higher playing field. There are a lot of people out there who can teach strategies, but that doesn't mean they can cultivate a strong mastermind group. You have to make sure they live by a certain level of ethics and values, and you want to make sure they surround themselves with the right people.

I always tell my mastermind clients,

"Don't copy what I do, copy how I think."

- *Structure is vital.* Most masterminds will meet virtually or in person during the year as a group. They'll also do group calls and some offer one-on-one coaching. Some may offer access to their programs, to other advisors, and to coaches. So, will their structure work for you and your lifestyle? The content and leader may be right, but if the structure doesn't work for you, then you have to find one that works for your lifestyle and your business.

- *The community matters.* The types of people from whom you can learn is also important—not just the mastermind leader, but the people in the group. Could they potentially support you? Could they inspire you? Could you partner with some of them? Are you inspired to be around that group or are you going to be the smartest person in the room? You know you don't want to join a mastermind where you're the smartest person in the room. It's okay if you're the smartest at one area of something, but you also want to learn from other people and make sure that there are really smart, talented people who are also thriving and successful in that room. If the facilitator is good at what they do, is strategic and specific about who they let in, this should take care of itself.

- *Accountability is necessary.* Most masterminds last from six months to a year. Is there accountability in place? Whether it's monthly or quarterly, are there milestones that allow you to set goals and create big results? By the end of the mastermind, you should be able to see incredible results. Your goals will determine what type of mastermind you will want to join. If you're looking for abundance of wealth and success in your industry or trying to scale or create something new, the mastermind you choose should support those goals. You want to have accountability in place to make sure you are set up for success. You need consistent accountability at the highest level. Is the mastermind that you want to be a part of creating that for you?

- *Coaching counts.* Your mastermind should make you think bigger and get out of your comfort zone. You don't want to join something that's going to keep you on the same level and maintain where you currently are. You may as well not do anything at all. You can maintain where you are at without any coaching, any inspiration, or any powerful mastermind group. You'll need to make sure the group you join can get you to the next level.

ARE YOU READY TO SHOW UP?

I believe you want to be a part of something that's pushing you to play bigger. As the Mel Robbins quote goes, "There will always be someone who can't see your worth. Don't let it be you." If you're ready to be uncomfortable and stop playing small or you feel like you're already the smartest person in the room, and if you're ready to participate in a whole new way, then you probably need a mastermind that will challenge you. This is what community gives you: the opportunity to bring work you care about to people eager to engage with it, pay you for it, and talk about it. I believe that the only way to make a real difference is to see and understand the people you seek to influence. Putting yourself in a community of like-minded people and allowing yourself to be coachable will change the questions you ask, the things you notice, and most of all, the work you're able to do. A mastermind will help you make things better by making better things. Your

work matters. You're going to want to work with and be surrounded by people you can learn from and who can help show
you a variety of new possibilities—who can help you get what
you want. If you are interested in learning more about SHINE
and how to apply for an invitation to my mastermind, you can
go to join.juliesolomon.net/shine.

CONCLUSION

Time to Get What You Want

I ONCE LED A GROUP in a yearlong coaching membership and made a huge mistake, which was a massive gift and learning experience. The mistake was that I inadvertently attracted some people who didn't have a purpose. And because they didn't have a purpose, there was nothing for them to lose. In a situation where you have nothing to lose, it's easy to quit. It's so easy to just kind of float around.

I had set up the offer like this: *Come and let me coach you. I will show you how to grow and scale your business. I'm going to give you a lot of my time and resources at a very affordable rate, and I'm not going to hold you to any sort of timeline. Month-to-month, no curriculum, no set schedule. Just come to me with your problems.*

That was a huge mistake—partially because it put all of the pressure to succeed on me, not on my clients where it should always be. This made me a less effective coach. As the months went on, I could tell many were not doing the work, and that they hadn't been focusing. They admitted that they were waiting for me to fix their problems.

And partially because of the way that I had set up the program and dynamic.

It was as if they were standing at the bottom of a ladder and I was right behind, urging, begging, and pleading for them to climb it. As they began their ascent, I propped myself behind them, pushing them up with all my might. With each unsteady step they took, I pushed all the harder. Eventually, when they lost their grip and fell, I fell, too, cushioning their blow.

As they got up and climbed again, I was right underneath, all the more concerned that they were holding on tight. Each time they slipped and tumbled, I fell beneath them and took the brunt once more. I began to notice that some of the clients weren't even holding on tightly or being careful with their footing. Why should they? They had fallen several times without sustaining injury. I was the one sustaining the injury. And we would all fall again.

Then I noticed that next to this ladder was another ladder with my name on it. I picked myself up off the ground, walked over, and began to climb it, finally feeling the freedom of my own climb, and the responsibility, success, and failure that came with it.

Even though I care about my clients, I realize that they must climb their own ladder by themselves. My attempts to help had only hindered their experience and results. As I climb my own ladder, I've discovered that I can't climb effectively while keeping an eye on the other ladder. So I focus on my own climb, and let my clients focus on theirs. If they fall, I will empathize, but I will not be injured. Their own injuries may help convince them to hold on tighter or learn a new way. Their success, or failure, and climbing out of the pit of failure, is their responsibility. Whether or not I climb is up to me.

So now, in my community, I say: "Come into this with me. I'm going to teach you a new way to think and connect you to some incredible people who will change your life, but if you don't do the work, if you don't trust the process, if you don't make a point to meet people and get the most out of this, then you won't get what you want. It's not my job to do it for you, nor is it my job to save you from your own resistance."

This approach has been far more loving and successful. It helps my clients create more impact and set up businesses that are stable and lucrative—businesses that bring them joy.

But if clients don't do what's necessary to help themselves, or are unwilling to take decisive action, then I don't work with them. Why? The most successful people I know are willing to show up and do the work. They take full responsibility for their own actions, and they are intensely motivated and grateful—for their lives, their opportunities, their successes, and even their failures. Which leads me to some concluding notes on gratitude.

GRATITUDE IS EVERYTHING

Part of success is knowing when you get what you want and being grateful for it. And part of success is cultivating perpetual gratitude. So many people don't pause in the moment of their success and recognize what they just achieved.

What happens once you get what you want? How do you truly take in the moment so that you're not chasing the next thing? Maybe you're not the breadwinner of your family, or maybe you are. Either way, I think a lot of people know what it feels like to be in that moment of, "We're at the finish line. We won! It's done. So what next?"

You can have limitless desires. How do we keep sight of the important moment of gratitude that must happen to cultivate more of the abundance in our lives?

Getting what you want and continuing to flow through each wave of that is all about you believing it's possible. Getting what we want should be this really beautiful, abundant, amazing thing.

We must not forget that getting what we want is a choice. And what a gift that is, because so many people don't even have the choice. My dad didn't have the choice I have. My mom didn't have the choice I have. Neither did their parents, nor theirs.

More than ever it is important to recognize that once you get what you want, you have to be grateful for it. And you have to savor the moment and celebrate your wins and recognize that it's perpetual.

You can use this over and over. You can read this book as many times as you want or find a community that supports you for all the things that you want. It's never just one and done. It's a constant evolution. Success is never a number. It's a feeling that is created by your thoughts. When you tap into the feeling, you're always getting what you want, because you're always grateful for what you have.

Remember, you are sourced from a greater source. You might not be able to control the support or lack of support from those around you, but what can you change? What can you shift? What's going to give you that feeling of being supported? Maybe it's a conversation with a friend or loved one. Maybe it's a walk outside. Maybe it's a hug from someone you love. It's your responsibility to stay grateful for what you have control over, and let go of the rest.

TRUST YOUR VISION

When you started reading this book, you had a sense of what you wanted. Perhaps you only knew what you absolutely didn't want. You picked this book up because you wanted something different out of life. You worked on aligning your purpose and creating a new vision for the future. This vision is yours and yours alone. You have all the tools now to go after that vision. You have a blueprint for what you need to do, clearly defined goals, and the skills and know-how to pitch, negotiate, and ask for what you want. You know how to leverage relationships, overcome your fears, and do the work to achieve the results you want. You are so close to living the life you've envisioned for yourself.

Now is the time to stay true to your new boundaries and hold them strong because you now know what you really want, you know what brings you joy and peace, and you have the strength to do whatever you want. Are you ready?

Ready is not a feeling. Ready is a decision.

It's time to continue to commit to your vision and commit to your routines because you're seeing big changes and bigger changes are coming. You also have new opportunities here. It's even normal for them to feel a little bit delayed because you're still working through it. I get it: it's hard work. And yes, it's a lot of work.

Some of you are thinking about changing your career. Making a big jump will bring you more opportunities and help you understand that you can achieve whatever you want. You're also going to find more peace. You can change the way you think and feel about the hustle culture. You don't need to hustle because now you know your worth.

All of us are going through sweeping life changes. The current "new normal" has fundamentally changed how all of us work, live, and think about the world. Many of us were literally forced to change overnight. Some of us lost our livelihoods, careers, loved ones, and even homes. Life as we know it changed at its core. Some of us even realized the person we love (who we suddenly had to spend 24-7 with) wasn't the person we were meant to be with, or the career to which we dedicated our life no longer provided the same satisfaction or joy. And while some of us loved the isolation and time to focus on ourselves, others longed for relationships, coworkers, and even their commutes. While many of us differed in our approach to how to deal, most of us figured out that we couldn't wait for someone else to come fix our problems for us. Most of us realized that if we wanted things to change, we had to be the ones to do the changing—mostly inside our minds and hearts. The pandemic, while it was grueling and brought untold suffering to many, had its silver linings. For one thing, it gave people so much time to take a good hard look at their life and what they wanted it to be in "the new normal"—or whatever came after it. This isn't the first time our world has seen major shifts. We have changed before, and we will change again. But I am confident that the tools I have shared in this book are evergreen. Whether you've chosen a life where working from home is for you, or you're busting at the seams to get back out into the world, the tools in this book will serve you no matter where you are. Whether at home, an office, or on a call, you will be able to live the life of your dreams and get what you want. Because when you say no to the people who don't want to respect your boundaries, who don't want to pay you properly, who don't want to treat you well, the world sees that you're growing and leveling up. You have a new vibration. The world will send you new people, new love, new collaborators, and new opportunities that will match that new vibration.

There are eight billion people in the world. You don't have to appeal to everyone, and please don't waste your time trying. You don't have to be everyone's solution provider. Let that false belief go. You will find another person who will match your vibration.

You can decide to leave. You can decide to say, "No, this is no longer for me."

Transformation brings death and a rebirth to all of our structures, our foundations, our supports. But don't worry if you don't know exactly what you want. Maybe you have a little bit of an idea, a sense of the direction, but not all the specifics. You don't really have a plan. You don't really feel ready. Don't rush it. You will have an opportunity to expand.

You don't need to do everything. The money, support, security—they're coming!

Whatever is truly yours, the universe wants you to have it. You won't miss it. It's not going to miss you and you don't need to force it.

You have the confidence. People want what you're offering. They are beginning to see you. They may even be admiring you. Just embrace that.

You have what you need. Enjoy everything you've built in this life.

There is a transition period that occurs when you step up to live as the real you. And creating change and making new things happen, really transforming yourself from the inside out? In that transition period you begin to step beyond the stories and the limitations that you once told yourself. You step beyond the illusion of who you thought you were, what you thought you could achieve, and what you thought was important. And instead, you become more of who you really are, that purposeful person who was always there. You're going to start to form new networks that are more aligned with your purpose and your values. Now, it does not mean that the new connections replace your existing group of people. It just means that your network will grow, and you will enrich your life with more love and more people. Those who knew you before might not get the new you. Yet others who have known you and always stayed with you on your path will embrace all your stages of growth.

You will meet people on the other side of your transformation who are going to be with you in that next phase. It's all great. It's all exactly how it's meant to be. The amazing thing about our world today is that there's really zero excuse for not having support for your dreams and your goals, because there are endless opportunities to connect with other like-minded people.

No matter how many unsupportive people there are in your life right now, remember there is truly only one voice to listen to. That voice is within you. Everything else is just noise.

YOUR TURN

I created a script for you that I'm about to share. You can use it to talk to your loved ones about your goals, about investing in your goals, and about how they can get on board to support you. Now, getting them on board is not your goal. Your goal is to stand in your power, own your truth, share your voice, and get what you want!

Hi, loved one, _____ is definitely an investment, but if I want my business to grow, if I want to make money, if I want to truly stand up and share my voice and contribute to the world, I can no longer stagnate. I really believe in my business/dream for my life, and I want it to succeed for myself and for our family. In order to do that, I can't stay stuck or alone anymore. I need to meet and work with others to share ideas, learn new strategies, get valuable feedback, and most important, make connections. I need to be in the right community. I need accountability and I want to be that for others as well. This is incredibly important to me. Can you get behind this?

Now can *you* get behind this? I mean, *really* get behind this. Are you ready to step into the light and shine? I think you are. You have all that it takes. Now get out there and get what you want!

EPILOGUE

I'M AT MY FAMILY BEACH house in Inlet Beach, Florida, for our annual summer vacation. I've been coming to the sandy beaches of 30A in the Florida panhandle for as long as I can remember. This place has borne witness to many iterations of my life. It's seen me single, married, divorced, and remarried. It has witnessed me young and alone, trying on many different masks to see what felt right.

Now it sees me being fully present, feeling aligned and balanced, living out my purpose while having fun with my family. As I sit here and gaze at the ocean, I'm so grateful for the business I've created that allows me to work while here if I want, while looking forward to new possibilities and new memories to come.

I also look forward to new possibilities and memories for you. I am proud of you and grateful you are here. I would love the chance to meet you someday in my mastermind, webinars, podcast community, or in person so we can share our own unique experience with one another. I know how hard it can be to hold strong to what's possible when the going gets tough.

A podcast listener once asked me, "Why isn't it enough to understand the concepts and strategies you teach? How much of this work do I have to do until this is done and I get what I want?" There was a long hesitation as I grappled with the complexity of trying to explain something that can be done, and done well, in a thousand different ways.

I told her this. We must change habits of behavior and thinking patterns that don't work and are actually self-destructive. Habits don't change just by reading about them. Even saying, "Yes, that's a habit I have," doesn't change it.

Challenges will keep coming up in different forms until you learn to choose differently.

Change comes through practicing something different. Doing this work for me means taking one of the many tools shared in this book and using it in my life. As I worked at making changes in myself, I found that where I used to react with frustration and helplessness, I now react with love and compassion, and it feels good. I am no longer a victim of life; I am a leader with choices. That vision allows me to live out my purpose and achieve freedom.

The suggestions in this book are your toolkit. But nothing changes until you change it. The toolkit just sits on the desk, like a pen waiting for the writer to take it up. Selecting the best tool requires some skill, but we are not lonely apprentices left to our own devices. We can ask for help, read books, call on our community, work with a coach, and test out suggestions on our own. As we practice, no lesson is lost, no experience is wasted, and more is revealed. We can help ourselves to any of the tools. We can go at our own pace.

Eventually, many of us realize that there is no quick fix or secret pill. It is my hope that you discover, just as I have, that there is always more to learn. It is also my hope that you will find support and peace not at the end of the journey, but along the way. Friends come along the way. Fun comes along the way. Challenges? There are always some of those along the way. Now at least we are equipped with new skills to help us meet those challenges. Finally, love, gratitude, and confidence also come along the way. These are the prime ingredients to getting exactly what you want.

ACKNOWLEDGMENTS

It took many people to make this book a reality. My literary agent and friend Margaret Riley King: thank you for always having my back. Thank you to Molly Kempf Hodgin for your direction and insight. To Sara Kendrick, Linda Alila, and Sicily Axton from HarperCollins Leadership, thank you for all you do.

A big thank you to Sarah Hall, Ashley Moreno, and the rest of the Sarah Hall Productions team.

Thank you, Mary Curran-Hackett. In addition to being a coach and editor, you became a true friend.

I am grateful for my parents' love and support, as well as for being part of a rich origin story from which I can learn and grow.

Johnathon, thank you for providing such amazing insight and reflection during this process. Thank you, Camden and Lily Jo, for being my forever inspiration.

Thank you, readers, for believing in what is possible.

INDEX

ABOUT THE AUTHOR

For more than fifteen years, Julie Solomon has been empowering lives—including her own. The host of the chart-topping *The Influencer Podcast*, Julie has launched several successful online coaching programs and services, including Pitch It Perfect, The Influencer Academy, SHINE Mastermind, and EmpowerYOU Membership. Through her work, she helps women turn messages into movements and empowers entrepreneurs to grow their influence and impact. Julie was recently named one of the Top 100 leaders in influencer marketing.

To learn more about Julie, visit www.juliesolomon.net.

A free, downloadable book study guide is available at
www.juliesolomon.net/bookresources.